GCSE
Mathematics:
Higher Level

Philip Hooper and Sheila Hunt

with Tony Buzan

Hodder & Stoughton

A MEMBER OF THE HODDER HEADLINE GROUP

ISBN 0 340 68860 2

First published 1997
Impression number   10 9 8 7 6 5 4 3 2 1
Year   2001 2000 1999 1998 1997

Designed and produced by Gecko Ltd, Bicester, Oxon
Printed in Great Britain for Hodder & Stoughton
Educational, a division of Hodder Headline Plc,
338 Euston Road, London NW1 3BH by Scotprint Ltd,
Musselburgh, Scotland.

Mind Maps: Philip Chambers
Illustrations: Karen Donnelly, Andrea Norton,
 Mike Parsons, John Plumb, Chris Rothero
Cover design: Amanda Hawkes
Cover illustration: Paul Bateman

Contents

Wanted – The Bodge City Bunch

By students looking for a decent grade.

Look out for

 Chief Icazaminna. He says, 'How!' (Well, he would, wouldn't he?) 'How to recognise ...', 'How to solve ...', 'How to revise ...' – in fact, 'How' to push your marks up to achieve that longed-for grade, and also 'How' to avoid blundering into

 the cow pats – Mathematical hazards lying in wait for the unwary

and 'How' to target the

 Tin Can Alley triplets, which mark a whole heap of Mathematical formulae.

His side-kicks, wanted in connection with Algebraic Activities, include

 Buffalo Lil,

 Chuckwagon Charlie, and

 Underhand Luke, three characters who, between them, have formula rearrangement all tied up, and

 Dino and Costas, the friendly bartenders at the Last Burp saloon, who will always offer a helping hand to anyone staggering through sequences.

Also wanted, and known to be quick on the draw, and involved in a host of previously unsolved Mathematical Mysteries:

 Sure Shot Stan your Dimensions Man and

 the X-Direct Duo, who will get all your problems into proportion.

The reward for anyone quick enough to pick up this gang could be impressive.

Reach for the Sky!

Revision made easy

The four pages that follow contain a gold mine of information on how you can achieve success both at school and in your exams. Read them and apply the information, and you will be able to spend less, but more efficient, time studying, with better results. If you already have another *Hodder & Stoughton Revision Guide*, skim-read these pages to remind yourself about the exciting new techniques the books use, then move ahead to page 1.

This section gives you vital information on how to remember more *while* you are learning and how to remember more *after* you have finished studying. It explains

how to use special techniques to improve your memory

how to use a revolutionary note-taking technique called Mind Maps that will double your memory and help you to write essays and answer exam questions

how to read everything faster while at the same time improving your comprehension and concentration

All this information is packed into the next four pages, so make sure you read them!

Your *amazing* memory

There are five important things you must know about your brain and memory to revolutionise your school life.

1 **how your memory ('recall') works *while* you are learning**

2 **how your memory works *after* you have finished learning**

3 **how to use Mind Maps – a special technique for helping you with all aspects of your studies**

4 **how to increase your reading speed**

5 **how to zap your revision**

1 Recall during learning – the need for breaks

When you are studying, your memory can concentrate, understand and remember well for between 20 and 45 minutes at a time. Then it *needs* a break. If you carry on for longer than this without one, your memory starts to break down! If you study for hours non-stop, you will remember only a fraction of what you have been trying to learn, and you will have wasted valuable revision time.

So, ideally, *study for less than an hour*, then take a five- to ten-minute break. During the break listen to music, go for a walk, do some exercise, or just daydream. (Daydreaming is a necessary brain-power booster – geniuses do it regularly.) During the break your brain will be sorting out what it has been learning, and you will go back to your books with the new information safely stored and organised in your memory banks. We recommend breaks at regular intervals as you work through the *Revision Guides*. Make sure you take them!

2 Recall after learning – the waves of your memory

What do you think begins to happen to your memory straight *after* you have finished learning something? Does It Immediately start forgetting? No! Your brain actually *increases* its power and carries on remembering. For a short time after your study session, your brain integrates the information, making a more complete picture of everything it has just learnt. Only then does the rapid decline in memory begin, and as much as 80 per cent of what you have learnt can be forgotten in a day.

However, if you catch the top of the wave of your memory, and briefly review (look back over) what you have been revising at the correct time, the memory is stamped in far more strongly, and stays at the crest of the wave for a much longer time. To maximise your brain's power to remember, take a few minutes and use a Mind Map to review what you have learnt at the end of a day. Then review it at the end of a week, again at the end of a month, and finally a week before the exams. That way you'll ride your memory wave all the way to your exam – and beyond!

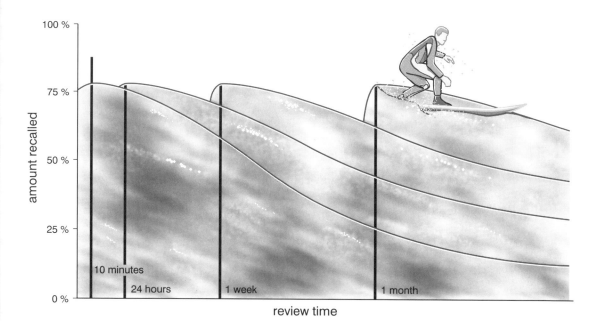

amount recalled

100 %

75 %

50 %

25 %

0 %

10 minutes

24 hours

1 week

1 month

review time

Amazing as your memory is (think of everything you actually do have stored in your brain at this moment) the principles on which it operates are very simple: your brain will remember if it (a) has an image (a picture or a symbol); (b) has that image fixed and (c) can link that image to something else.

3 The Mind Map® – a picture of the way you think

Do you *like* taking notes? More importantly, do you like having to go back over and learn them before exams? Most students I know certainly do not! And how do you take your notes? Most people take notes on lined paper, using blue or black ink. The result, visually, is *boring*! And what does your brain do when it is bored? It turns off, tunes out, and goes to sleep! Add a dash of colour, rhythm, imagination, and the whole note-taking process becomes much more fun, uses more of your brain's abilities, *and* improves your recall and understanding.

A Mind Map mirrors the way your brain works. It can be used for note-taking from books or in class, for reviewing what you have just studied, for revising, and for essay planning for coursework and in exams. It uses all your memory's natural techniques to build up your rapidly growing 'memory muscle'.

You will find Mind Maps throughout this book. Study them, add some colour, personalise them, and then have a go at drawing your own – you'll remember them far better! Put them on your walls and in your files for a quick-and-easy review of the topic.

How to draw a Mind Map

● Start in the middle of the page with the page turned sideways. This gives your brain the maximum room for its thoughts.

● Always start by drawing a small picture or symbol. Why? Because a picture is worth a thousand words to your brain. And try to use at least three colours, as colour helps your memory even more.

● Let your thoughts flow, and write or draw your ideas on coloured branching lines connected to your central image. These key symbols and words are the headings for your topic. The Mind Map at the top of the next page shows you how to start.

● Then add facts and ideas by drawing more, smaller, branches on to the appropriate main branches, just like a tree.

● Always print your word clearly on its line. Use only one word per line. The Mind Map at the foot of the

next page shows you how to do this.

● To link ideas and thoughts on different branches, use arrows, colours, underlining, and boxes.

How to read a Mind Map

● Begin in the centre, the focus of your topic.

● The words/images attached to the centre are like chapter headings, read them next.

● Always read out from the centre, in every direction (even on the left-hand side, where you will have to read from right to left, instead of the usual left to right).

Using Mind Maps

Mind Maps are a versatile tool – use them for taking notes in class or from books, for solving problems, for brainstorming with friends, and for reviewing and revising for exams – their uses are endless! You will find them invaluable for planning essays for coursework and exams. Number your main branches in the order in which you want to use them and off you go – the main headings for your essay are done and all your ideas are logically organised!

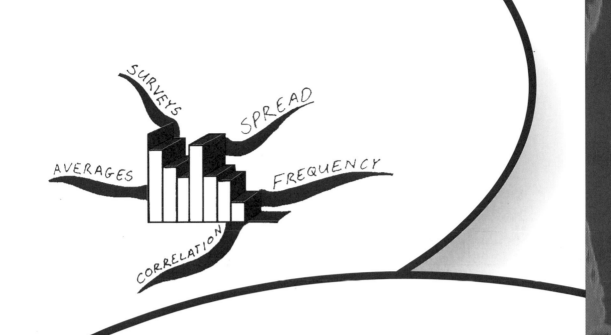

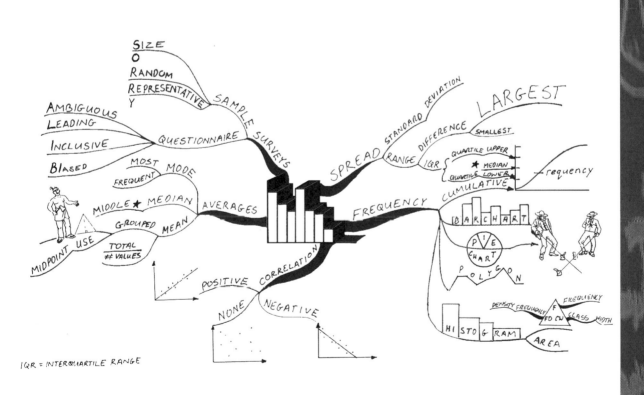

IQR = INTERQUARTILE RANGE

4 Super speed reading

It seems incredible, but it's been proved – the faster you read, the more you understand and remember! So here are some tips to help you to practise reading faster – you'll cover the ground more quickly, remember more, *and* have more time for revision!

★ Read the whole text (whether it's a lengthy book or an exam paper) very quickly first, to give your brain an overall idea of what's ahead and get it working. (It's like sending out a scout to look at the territory you have to cover – it's much easier when you know what to expect!) Then read the text again for more detailed information.

★ Have the text a reasonable distance away from your eyes. In this way your eye/brain system will be able to see more at a glance, and will naturally begin to read faster.

★ Take in groups of words at a time. Rather than reading slowly and 'carefully' read faster, more enthusiastically. Your comprehension will rocket!

★ Take in phrases rather than single words while you read.

★ Use a guide. Your eyes are designed to follow movement, so a thin pencil underneath the lines you are reading, moved smoothly along, will 'pull' your eyes to faster speeds.

5 Helpful hints for exam revision

Start to revise at the beginning of the course. Cram at the start, not the end and avoid 'exam panic'!

Use Mind Maps throughout your course, and build a Master Mind Map for each subject – a giant Mind Map that summarises everything you know about the subject.

Use memory techniques such as mnemonics (verses or systems for remembering things like dates and events, or lists).

Get together with one or two friends to revise, compare Mind Maps, and discuss topics.

And finally...

● *Have fun while you learn* – studies show that those people who enjoy what they are doing understand and remember it more, and generally do it better.

● *Use your teachers* as resource centres. Ask them for help with specific topics and with more general advice on how you can improve your all-round performance.

● *Personalise your Revision Guide* by underlining and highlighting, by adding notes and pictures. Allow your brain to have a conversation with it!

Your brain is an amazing piece of equipment – learn to use it, and you, like thousands of students before you will be able to master 'B's and 'A's with ease. The more you understand and use your brain, the more it will repay you!

What's 'hard' about Maths

1 ✗ There's so much to do.

  ✔ Don't worry! The techniques used in this book will drastically reduce the amount of time you need to spend on your Maths revision.

2 ✗ I can't revise Maths.

  ✔ You can with our book. Although we've kept it short, we've included plenty of examples and loads of practice in the sorts of questions that you'll get in the exam.

3 ✗ I can never understand what Maths books are saying.

  ✔ You don't need a degree in Maths-speak to understand our book. We use everyday language as far as possible, and we explain any complicated terms so that you too can show off by using them yourself.

4 ✗ I can't remember all those complicated methods.

  ✔ Oh yes you can, because we have slaved away thinking up simple, easily remembered ways of recalling all that knowledge which you have so painfully acquired.

5 ✗ Why didn't I buy this book before?

  ✔ Better late than never!

RULES

FOR USING THIS BOOK

Here are the rules for using this book.

Pay attention to them and learn them well.

Rule 1 – There are no rules!

You do not have to begin at Chapter 1, then go on to Chapter 2, and so on. You may want to start with the topics you find easiest. If you feel supremely confident, you may jump to the end of the chapter, where you will find exam-style questions.

Alternatively, you may want to kick off by tackling the topics you find toughest.

Each chapter contains new approaches to solving Maths problems, which are designed to be easy to remember. If this book is your own, treat it as such – feel free to draw in it and makes notes or comments to help you.

Above all, enjoy using it!

Throughout this book our Wild West characters will be there to help you understand and remember.

Philip Hooper and Sheila Hunt

Types of number

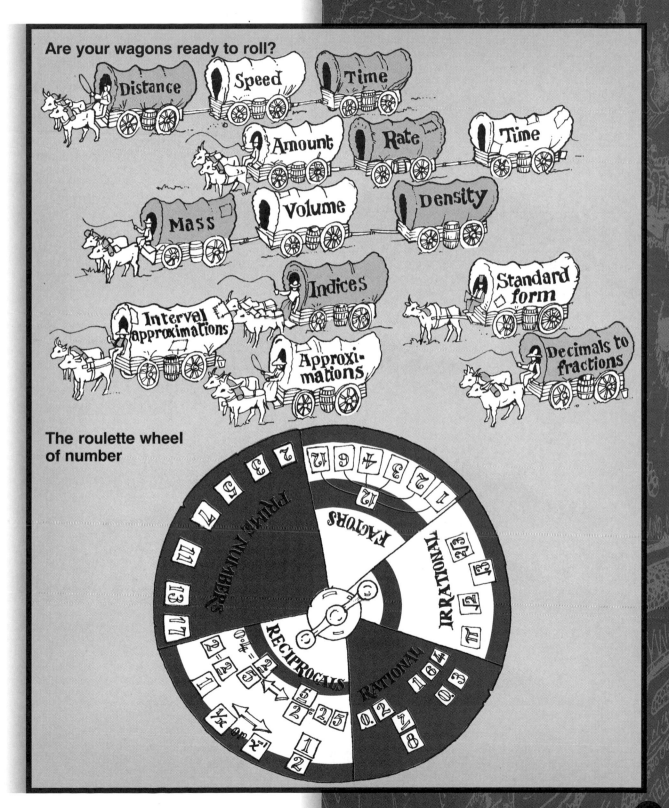

Are your wagons ready to roll?

The roulette wheel of number

preview

By the end of this chapter you will be able to:

- **identify the different types of numbers**

- **manipulate rational and irrational numbers**

- **evaluate an unknown by substituting given values into a formula**

- **approximate and round to the nearest unit**

- **identify the interval in which the value of a rounded figure may fall**

- **simplify expressions involving indices, including negative and fractional indices**

- **express a large or a small number in standard form**

- **convert decimals to fractions and vice versa**

- **express recurring decimals as fractions**

Don't tread in the cowpats!

Whenever you see this sign – take care.

Remember: you have been warned!

Factors, primes and rational numbers

Factors are numbers which 'divide into' other numbers.

For example 6 is a factor of 12, 5 is a factor of 40.

Prime numbers can only be divided by themselves and 1. In other words, they have exactly 2 factors, themselves and 1.

Note that 1 is not a prime number.

Prime factors are prime numbers which are factors of another number.

For example 6 is a factor of 12, but 5 is a prime factor of 40.

Reciprocals are the numbers you get by turning another number 'upside-down'. With whole numbers this becomes '1 over' the number.

On a calculator this is the key marked `1/x` or `x⁻¹`.

For example:

$$2 = \frac{2}{1}$$ 　　　　The reciprocal is $\frac{1}{2}$

　　　　　　　　　　(or 0.5 on the calculator)

$$2.5 = 2\tfrac{1}{2} = \frac{5}{2}$$ 　　The reciprocal is $\frac{2}{5}$ or 0.4

Rational numbers are numbers which can be represented as:

- integers (whole numbers)

- fractions

- finite or terminating decimals (i.e. decimals that do not go on for ever)

- recurring decimals.

Irrational numbers

Irrational numbers are all numbers which are not rational!

When an irrational number is written as a decimal, it goes on and on indefinitely, without any pattern.

The main types you will see are:

- π

- square roots of non-square numbers. e.g. $\sqrt{2}$, $\sqrt{5}$

The words 'rational' and 'irrational' have the same origins as the word 'ratio'. Any rational number can be written as a ratio (or fraction). Even an integer or whole number can be written as a ratio, for example:

$4 = \dfrac{4}{1}$

How to change an irrational number to a rational number

Addition or subtraction

Example 1.1

What must be added to $1 + \sqrt{2}$ to make a rational number?

Solution

The irrational part of $1 + \sqrt{2}$ is the $\sqrt{2}$. To get rid of the irrational part, add $-\sqrt{2}$.

Multiplication

Example 1.2

What number, other than $\sqrt{2}$, can be multiplied by $\sqrt{2}$ to give a rational number?

Solution

$2\sqrt{2}$ is one possibility. Although it looks the same as $\sqrt{2}$, it is a different number.

$2\sqrt{2} \times \sqrt{2} = 4$ because $\sqrt{2} \times \sqrt{2} = 2$

Another solution is to find a square number that has 2 as a factor.
Take 16, then take a factor of 2 out, leaving 8.

As $\sqrt{2} \times \sqrt{8} = \sqrt{16} = 4$, the answer could be $\sqrt{8}$.

Note that $\sqrt{2 \times 8} = \sqrt{2} \times \sqrt{8}$ but $\sqrt{2 + 8}$ is not the same as $\sqrt{2} + \sqrt{8}$.

Exercise 1.1

1 Are the following numbers rational or irrational?
   a) 2π **b)** $\sqrt{2} \times \sqrt{50}$ **c)** $\sqrt{289}$ **d)** $\dfrac{1}{\sqrt{5}}$
   e) $\sqrt{2} + \sqrt{2}$

2 What number can be multiplied by $\sqrt{5}$ to give a rational product? Express your answer in the form $\sqrt{a}$, where a is a rational integer other than 5.

3 If $\dfrac{1}{x} = 0.2$, find x.

Answers

3 5

2 Either $x\sqrt{5}$, where x is an integer e.g. $2\sqrt{5}$, or a number of the form $\sqrt{5x^2}$ e.g. $\sqrt{20}$

1 **a)** irrational **b)** rational **c)** rational **d)** irrational **e)** irrational

Formulae

Meet the Tin Can Alley triplets

The Tin Can Alley triplets help you to remember formulae, which are used in lots of questions throughout this book.

To find a letter, firstly cover it up. If the uncovered letters are:

* on the same level, multiply them, or

* on different levels, divide the top by the bottom.

Distance, Speed, Time

$$D = S \times T \qquad S = \frac{D}{T} \qquad T = \frac{D}{S}$$

Remember **D**owning **St**.

You may have used S for distance and V or v for velocity in place of speed. If so, you need **S**atellite **TV**, in the form:

$$S = T \times V \qquad T = \frac{S}{V} \qquad V = \frac{S}{T}$$

Amount, Rate, Time

$$A = R \times T \qquad R = \frac{A}{T} \qquad T = \frac{A}{R}$$

Density formula

This is **M**aths for the **V**ery **D**ense!

$$M = V \times D \qquad V = \frac{M}{D} \qquad D = \frac{M}{V}$$

mass = volume $\times$ density ($M = V \times D$) etc.

Example 1.3

The Transaridzona Express travels at 45 km/h. How far does it travel in 3 hours and 25 minutes?

You may see speeds such as 45 km/h expressed in other ways, such as 45 km per hour, or 45 km h^{-1}. They all mean the same thing.

Solution

Firstly, do not write 3 hours 25 minutes as 3.25.

3 hours 25 minutes = $3 + \frac{25}{60}$ or 3 $\boxed{a^{b/c}}$ 25 $\boxed{a^{b/c}}$ 60

You are asked for the distance. Cover or cross out D.

S and T are on the same level, so you multiply them.

$D = S \times T$

$\quad = 45 \times 3 \lrcorner 25 \lrcorner 60$

$\quad = 153.75\,\text{km}$

Remember that distances are usually given in decimals.

Example 1.4

Beer is poured from a barrel at a rate of $25\,\text{cm}^3$ per second. How long does it take to fill a 1 litre jug? (1 litre = $1000\,\text{cm}^3$)

Solution

$T = \dfrac{A}{R} = \dfrac{1000}{25} = 40$ seconds

Don't mix units.
Convert litres into cm^3 before you start a question like this.

Example 1.5

Chief Sitting Duck's horse travels 36 kilometres in 1 hour and 30 minutes. Find its average speed in kilometres per hour.

Solution

$S = \dfrac{D}{T} = 24\,\text{km/h}$

Did you get the right answer? If you didn't it's probably because you wrote the time as 1.30 instead of 1 hour 30 minutes = 1.5 hours.

Exercise 1.2

1 The Old Mule Express can carry post 120 kilometres in 5 hours and 15 minutes. How fast does it go?

2 A group of men can unload grain at the rate of 6 cubic metres per hour. How long does it take them to unload 44 cubic metres? Give your answer in hours and minutes.

3 Duck feathers weighing 0.81 kg are packed into a box of volume 54 000 cubic centimetres. Find the density of the feathers, in g/cm^3.

3 $0.015\,\text{g/cm}^3$
2 7.3 hours = 7 hours 20 minutes
1 22.9 km/h

Answers

TAKE A BREAK

When you come back, it'll be about time for some approximations.

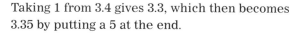
Approximation

Rounding

Remember, when you round:

if the last digit is 0, 1, 2, 3 or 4 you ignore it,

if the last digit is 5, 6, 7, 8 or 9 you round up.

When you are using decimal places or significant figures, the above rules apply, but always read the question carefully. If, for instance, your answer suggests that 5.2 wagons are required to carry a certain number of people, you will probably need to round up to 6 to avoid stranded passengers!

If your final answer requires, say, two decimal places, either use your calculator's memory or else round to four decimal places until you need the final answer, to avoid inaccuracies.

Approximation to the nearest unit
Rounding errors

Example 1.6

If a number, rounded to one decimal place, becomes 3.4:

3.3   3.35   3.4   3.45   3.5

what is the possible range of the original number?

Strictly, the original number could be anywhere between 3.35, the lower bound, and 3.449 99 ..., the upper bound. However, when dealing with this type of question, we take the upper bound as 3.45.

Solution

Method 1
To find the upper bound, you simply put a 5 at the end of the decimal.

To find the lower bound, you subtract 1 from the last digit and put a 5 at the end.

Taking 1 from 3.4 gives 3.3, which then becomes 3.35 by putting a 5 at the end.

Upper bound = 3.45

Lower bound = 3.35

Method 2
Write the number you are given.

Put zero beneath each digit after the decimal point, then put a 5 at the end. This creates a new number which you must subtract to get the lower bound and add to get the upper bound.

i.e.   3.4

    0.05

Taking away: 3.4 – 0.05 gives 3.35, the lower bound.

Adding: 3.4 + 0.05 gives 3.45, the upper bound.

Interval approximation

An interval approximation is simply a way of writing the lower and upper bounds. Your answer will contain one more digit than the number in the question. Interval approximation is the opposite of rounding.

Example 1.7

Write, as an interval approximation, 6.13 correct to 2 d.p.

Solution

A question like this requires as answer containing three decimal places, although at first glance it seems to ask for two.

6.13

0.005

Lower bound: 6.13 – 0.005 = 6.125

Upper bound: 6.13 + 0.005 = 6.135

Calculating rounding errors

Remember that the larger the number you divide by, the smaller the answer, and vice versa.

Example 1.8

The area of a rectangular field is 42 200 m², and its length is 278 m, both correct to three significant figures. Find the greatest and smallest possible breadths of the field, correct to one decimal place.

Solution

The interval approximation of the length is 277.5 to 278.5.

The interval approximation for the area is 42 150 to 42 250

The largest breadth is

$$\frac{\text{largest area}}{\text{smallest length}} = \frac{42\,250}{277.5} = 152.3 \text{ m}$$

The smallest possible breadth is

$$\frac{\text{smallest area}}{\text{largest length}} = \frac{42\,150}{278.5} = 151.3 \text{ m}$$

Exercise 1.3

1 Ten cameras in a box each weigh 1.2 kg to the nearest 0.1 kg. Find the lower and upper bounds for the weight of the ten cameras.

2 A pencil is found to measure 18 cm to the nearest cm. What is the longest possible length of the pencil?

3 The area of a rectangle is given as 14.1 cm² to the nearest 0.1 cm² and its width is given as 6.2 cm to the nearest 0.1 cm. Calculate the upper and lower bounds of its length.

4 Write, as an interval approximation, 3.24, correct to 2 d.p.

Answers

1 11.5 and 12.5 kg   **2** 18.5 cm   **3** 2.30 cm and 2.25 cm   **4** 3.235, 3.245

TAKE A BREAK

The indications are that you're about ready for another break!

Indices

In the number 2^3, the 3 is called the **power** or the **index**. The plural of index is indices.

2^3 means 3 lots of 2 multiplied together or $2 \times 2 \times 2$ **not** 2×3.

$2^{\frac{1}{2}}$ means $\sqrt{2}$ and $2^{\frac{1}{3}}$ means $\sqrt[3]{2}$.

Rules

1 *You can only simplify indices when the base number is the same.*

2 *When dividing or multiplying powers of the same number remember TIP and DIM.*

    TIP   *Times = **I**ndices **P**lus*
    DIM   *Divide = **I**ndices **M**inus*

Example 1.9

Simplify these by expressing them as a power of 3.

a) $3^2 \times 3^5$ b) $3^7 \div 3^2$ c) $3^2 + 3^5$
d) $3^5 \times 2^3$ e) $3^3 \div 3^2$

Solution

a) $3^2 \times 3^5 = 3^7$

b) $3^7 \div 3^2 = 3^5$

c) $3^2 + 3^5$ Cannot be simplified as a power of 3.

d) $3^5 \times 2^3$ Cannot be simplified because the base numbers are different.

e) $3^3 \div 3^2 = 3$

Negative and fractional indices

A negative power means '1 over' (or a **reciprocal**).

$$x^{-2} = \frac{1}{x^2}$$

A fractional index indicates a root.

$$x^{\frac{1}{2}} = \sqrt{x} \qquad x^{\frac{1}{3}} = \sqrt[3]{x} \qquad x^{\frac{2}{3}} = \sqrt[3]{x^2}$$

Example 1.10

Evaluate $9^3 \div 9^5$.

Express your answer:

a) as a power of 9

b) as a fraction.

Solution

a) $9^3 \div 9^5 = 9^{-2}$

b) $9^{-2} = \dfrac{1}{9^2} = \dfrac{1}{81}$

Exercise 1.4

1 Simplify $3^2 \times 3^5$, giving your answer as a power of 3.

2 Simplify $3^2 \div 3^5$, giving your answer:
a) as a power of 3   **b)** as a fraction.

3 Write $4^{-\frac{1}{2}}$ as a fraction.

4 Simplify $(x \times x^5) \div \sqrt{x}$.

5 Write $\dfrac{\sqrt{x}}{yz^2}$ in the form $x^a y^b z^c$.

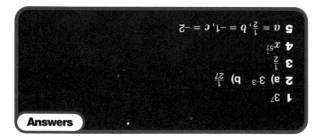

5 $a = \frac{1}{2}, b = -1, c = -2$
4 $x^{\frac{9}{2}}$
3 $\frac{1}{2}$
2 a) 3^{-3} **b)** $\frac{1}{27}$
1 3^7

Answers

Standard form or standard index form

This is a short method of writing very large or very small numbers.

$10^1 = 10$ $10^{-1} = 0.1$

$10^2 = 100$ $10^{-2} = 0.01$

$10^3 = 1000$ $10^{-3} = 0.001$

$10^8 = 100\,000\,000$ and so on.

Example 1.11

Write $34\,200$ in standard form.

Solution

$$\begin{aligned} 34\,200 &= 3420 \times 10 \\ &= 342 \times 100 \\ &= 34.2 \times 1000 \\ &= 3.42 \times 10\,000 \end{aligned}$$

Written in standard form, $34\,200$ becomes 3.42×10^4.

Example 1.12

Write $0.000\,067$ in standard form.

Solution

$0.000\,067 = 6.7 \times 10^{-5}$

Check on your calculator if you are in any doubt.

3.42×10^4 [3] [.] [4] [2] [EXP] [4] [=]

6.7×10^{-5} [6] [.] [7] [EXP] [5] [+/−] [=]

On some calculators, you will find [EE] instead of [EXP].

If your calculator does not change the standard form number into its equivalent, try doing it the other way round: i.e. enter $0.000\,067$ and press [=].

If you can say, 'times 10 to the,' replace it with EXP or EE.

Do not press ✕ 1 0 EXP

TAKE A BREAK

This is another good place to take a break, before starting the dash for the end of the chapter.

Using your calculator

Examiners often set questions like:

Solve $\dfrac{\sqrt{31.92}}{51.7 - 7.3^2}$

It is important to remember that your calculator will square or take the square root, then multiply or divide, then add or subtract. Using brackets and sometimes = *you can change this order.*

Example 1.13

Evaluate $\dfrac{18 + 2}{5}$

Solution

You can see that the answer is $20 \div 5 = 4$, but if you keyed in $18 + 2 \div 5$ your calculator would show 18.4, as it would calculate $2 : 5$ before adding the 18.

You can avoid this by keying in:

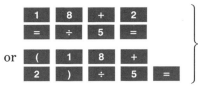

```
1  8  +  2
=  ÷  5  =
```
or
```
(  1  8  +
2  )  ÷  5  =
```
to give the answer, 4

Either way the 18 and the 2 are added before you divide.

Example 1.14

Evaluate $\dfrac{60 + \sqrt{5}}{7.2 - 3.1}$

Solution

$\dfrac{60 + \sqrt{5}}{7.2 - 3.1} = (60 + \sqrt{5}) \div (7.2 - 3.1) = 15.2$

Exercise 1.5

1 Evaluate $\dfrac{\sqrt{7} + 12}{3.4^2 - 6.1}$

2 Evaluate $\dfrac{1}{\sqrt{3} + \sqrt{5}}$

3 Evaluate $f = \dfrac{xy}{\sqrt{x - y}}$ where $x = 3.7$ and $y = -0.2$.

4 Find an approximate answer to $\dfrac{3.8 \times 7.9}{0.18 + 1.8}$ showing all your working.

Answers

4 $(4 \times 8) \div (0.2 + 1.8) = 32 \div 2 = 16$
3 -0.37
2 0.25
1 2.68

Make sure you know the difference between the x^y (or y^x) and EXP or EE buttons on your calculator.

Converting decimals to fractions

Finite or terminating decimals may be converted as follows.

$0.3 = \frac{3}{10}$ $0.14 = \frac{14}{100}$ $0.986 = \frac{986}{1000}$

Recurring or non-terminating decimals

Example 1.15

Write 0.333 333 3... as a fraction in its lowest terms.

Solution

As there is only one repeating digit, multiply both sides by 10 initially.

Let $x = 0.333\,333\,3...$ **1**

$10x = 3.333\,333...$ **2**

$9x = 3$ subtracting **2 – 1**

$x = \frac{3}{9} = \frac{1}{3}$

Example 1.16

Write 0.141 414... as a fraction.

Solution

As there is a pattern of two repeating digits, multiply through by 100 which is 10^2.

$x = 0.141\,414...$ **1**

$100x = 14.1414....$ **2**

$99x = 14$ subtracting **2 – 1**

$x = \frac{14}{99}$

Summary of the method

Multiply your original decimal by a power of 10, depending on the pattern of repeats in the decimal.

Where one number is repeated in the decimal, multiply by 10 (or 10^1).

For example, 0.555 555 55... or 0.222 222 2...

Where two numbers are repeated, multiply by 100 (or 10^2).

For example 0.434 343 43... or 0.767 676 76...

Where three numbers are repeated, multiply by 1000 (or 10^3).

For example 0.231 231 231 231... or 0.953 953 953 953...

The 999 method (a quicker way)

If you have a single digit which is repeated, such as 0.333 33..., this can be expressed as a digit over 9.

For example $0.333\,33... = \frac{3}{9} = \frac{1}{3}$ or $0.888\,88... = \frac{8}{9}$

If two numbers are repeated in the decimal, then the decimal can be expressed as the same two numbers over 99.

For example $0.878\,787\,87.... = \frac{87}{99} = \frac{29}{33}$ or $0.636\,363\,63... = \frac{63}{99} = \frac{7}{11}$

Similarly for a repeating group of three digits.

For example $0.145\,145\,145... = \frac{145}{999}$ or $0.123\,123\,123... = \frac{123}{999} = \frac{41}{333}$

If you have a recurring decimal that starts with a few different digits that are followed by repeating numbers, such as 0.123 333..., you will need to modify this method.

$0.123\,333\,33... = 0.333\,333\,3... - 0.21$

$$= \frac{3}{9} - \frac{21}{100}$$

$$= \frac{37}{300} \text{ (Check, using your calculator.)}$$

Exercise 1.6

1 Write each of these numbers as a fraction.
     a) 0.242 424 242...   **b)** 0.562 424 242...

2 Write 0.345 345 345... as a fraction.

3 If $x = 0.516\,516\,516...$, evaluate:

     a) $1000x$ **b)** $999x$

     c) x as a rational number in the form $\dfrac{a}{b}$.

Answers

3 a) 516.516 516 516...   **b)** 516   **c)** $\frac{172}{333}$

2 $\frac{115}{333}$

1 a) $\frac{8}{33}$ **b)** $\frac{464}{825}$

TAKE A BREAK

Take another break to gather your strength for some hard work!

Playtime's over!

Exam-type questions 1

1 Write 5300 as an interval approximation correct to 3 sig. figs.

2 Evaluate the following.

a) $\dfrac{12.76 - 4.71}{4.90 + 1.77}$

b) $\dfrac{11.1^2}{\sqrt{9.4 - 2.1}}$

c) $\dfrac{5.6}{(1.9 - 0.7)^2}$

3 A particle travels 1.75 m in 1.26 seconds.
  a) What is its speed in m/s?
  b) What is its speed in km per hour?
  c) Assuming that the given information has been rounded to 3 sig. figs., find the upper and lower bounds of its speed, in m/s.

4 Use the formula $V = \frac{1}{4}\pi xy\sqrt{x^2 - 2y^2}$ to find V when $x = 1.4$ and $y = 0.6$.

5 Give two different irrational numbers in the form $\sqrt{a}$ and $\sqrt{b}$ that can be multiplied together to give a rational answer.

6 The number 2.38 has been written correct to 2 d.p. State its lower and upper bounds.

7 The speed of light is approximately 3×10^8 m/s. Find the time it takes in minutes for it to travel 7.2×10^{10} metres.

8 The mass of an object is 1750 grams, correct to 3 sig. figs. Its volume is 272 cm^3 correct to 3 sig. figs. Find the upper and lower bounds of its density, stating the units.

9 Find a number, other than $\sqrt{5}$, which can be multiplied by $\sqrt{5}$ to give a rational answer.

10 Use the formula $C = \dfrac{a + b}{a - b^2}$ to find C when $a = -41.7$ and $b = 32.6$. Give your answer correct to 3 sig. figs.

11 Are the following numbers rational or irrational?
  a) $\frac{1}{\pi}$ **b)** $\sqrt{3} \times \sqrt{12}$ **c)** $\sqrt{5} + \sqrt{5}$ **d)** $(\sqrt{7})^2$ **e)** $\frac{2}{5}$

12 Express each of the following in the form $\dfrac{a}{b}$ where a and b are integers.
  a) 0.666…   **b)** 0.720 720 720…
  c) 0.213 333 333 3…

13 If $x = 0.162\,162\,162\ldots$ find:
  a) $1000x$ **b)** $999x$
  c) Express x as a fraction in its lowest terms.

14 Simplify the following where possible.
  a) $27^{-\frac{1}{3}}$ expressing your answer as a fraction
  b) $\dfrac{5^{-2} \times 5^3}{\sqrt{5}}$ giving your answer as a power of 5
  c) $3^2 + 3^4$
  d) $25 \div 5^4$ giving your answer **i)** as a power of 5, **ii)** as a fraction.

15 a) Give an example of a rational number between $\sqrt{24}$ and $\sqrt{26}$.
  b) Give an example of an irrational number between 9 and 10.

Answers

1 5295, 5305

2 a) 1.21   **b)** 45.6   **c)** 3.9

3 a) 1.39 m/s   **b)** 5 km/h
  c) 1.755 ÷ 1.255 = 1.40, 1.745 ÷ 1.265 = 1.38

4 0.73 correct to 2 d.p.

5 Find a square number which has 2 as a factor, express it as a product of two factors, such as 36, because $\sqrt{2} \times \sqrt{18} = \sqrt{36}$.

6 2.375, 2.385

7 $(7.2 \times 10^{10}) \div (3 \times 10^8) = 240$ seconds $= 4$ minutes

8 1755 ÷ 271.5 = 6.46 g/cm^3, 1745 ÷ 272.5 = 6.40 g/cm^3

9 Find a square number that has 5 as a factor, such as 100, because $\sqrt{5} \times \sqrt{20} = \sqrt{100}$, or $5\sqrt{5}$; see answer to question 5

10 0.008 24

11 a) irrational   **b)** rational   **c)** irrational
  d) rational   **e)** rational

12 a) $\frac{2}{3}$ **b)** $\frac{80}{111}$ **c)** $\frac{16}{75}$

13 a) 162.162 162…   **b)** 162   **c)** $\frac{6}{37}$

14 a) $\frac{1}{3}$ **b)** $5^{\frac{1}{2}}$ **c)** cannot be simplified as a power of 3.
  d) i) 5^{-2} **ii)** $\frac{1}{25}$

15 a) e.g. 5
  b) the root of any number between 82 and 99, e.g. $\sqrt{90}$.

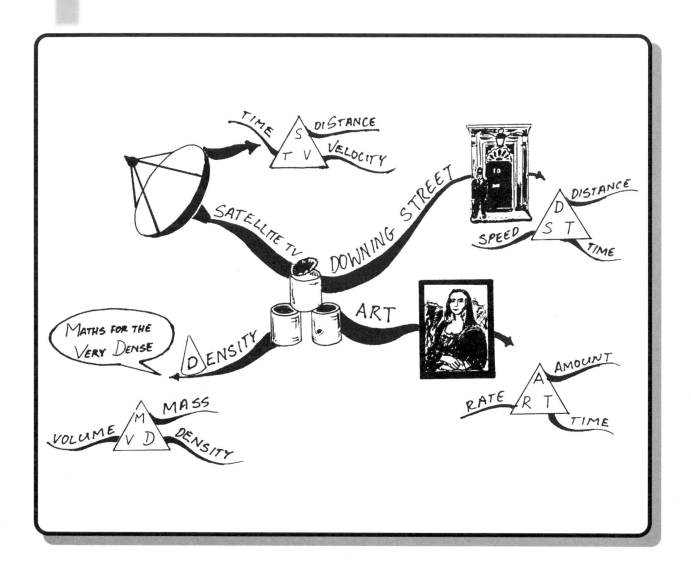

review
How much have you learnt?

Tick off each topic in the list when you are confident you can cope with it.

○ Identify the different types of numbers
rational
irrational.

○ Manipulate rational and irrational numbers.

○ Evaluate an unknown by substituting given values into a formula.

○ Approximate and round to the nearest unit.

○ Identify the interval in which the value of a rounded figure may fall.

○ Simplify expressions involving indices, including negative and fractional indices.

○ Express a large or a small number in standard form.

○ Convert decimals to fractions and vice versa.

○ Express recurring decimals as fractions.

roportion lity and percentages

2

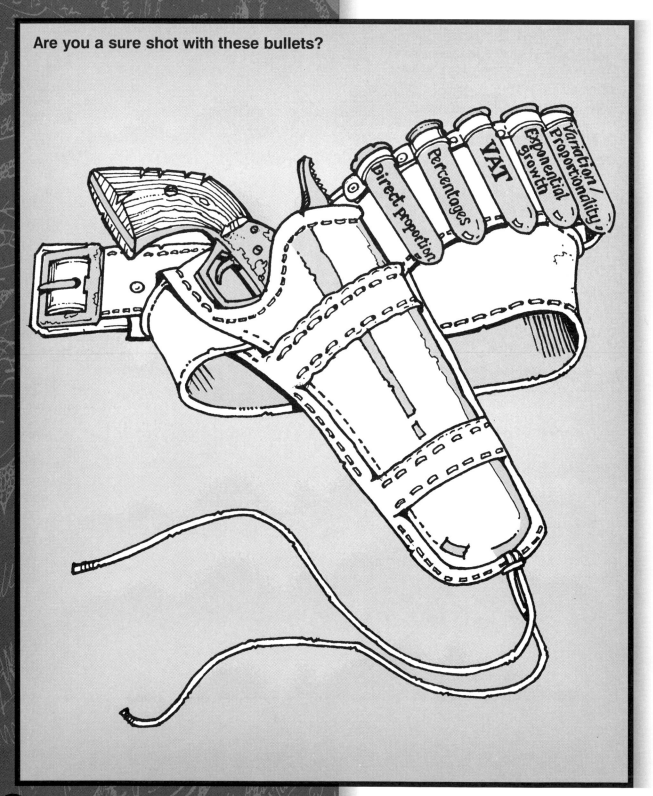

Are you a sure shot with these bullets?

Direct proportion

Percentages

VAT

Exponential growth

Variation / Proportionality

preview

By the end of this chapter you will be able to:

- **answer questions on ratio and proportion**

- **work out a percentage of a number**

- **express one number as a percentage of another**

- **solve problems involving VAT**

- **work out problems involving exponential growth or decay**

- **find constants of proportionality in questions on variation**

- **simplify ratios**

Would you like one quick and easy method guaranteed to solve all these questions?

1 If 74 members of the Havago tribe fire 333 arrows in 5 minutes, how many arrows could 52 members fire in the same time and at the same rate?

2 In 1862 the population of Bodge City increased by 15%, or 252 people. What was the population in 1861?

3 A pie chart represents 300 members of the Putemup tribe. How many degrees represent 80 members?

4 If the Last Burp Saloon offered 126 poker chips for 4.5 nuggets of gold, how many nuggets would be received from 350 chips?

Did you spot Chief Icazaminna on page 7? Wherever he pops up you know he is telling you 'How'!

Introducing X-Direct with Bodge City's fastest draws, Tim Times and David Divide

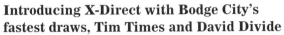

We'll show you our method using a really easy example so that you can see how it works.

Really Easy Example!

Example 2.1

Five buffalo cost $15. Find the cost of seven buffalo.

Solution

This is probably the method you used in the past.

5 cost $15

1 costs $15 ÷ 5 = £3

7 cost $3 × 7 = £21

X-Direct Method
Step 1 Set out the information in a table.

	Buffalo	Cost ($)
What does the question tell me?	5	15
What do I need to know?	7	

Make sure you put the numbers under the right heading!

Step 2

Buffalo   Cost ($)

5 ⟍⟋ 15

7 ⟋⟍

Draw in the diagonal X as shown.

Now apply X-Direct.

Tim (the better shot) hits two numbers, and David gets only one number.

For Tim's two numbers you 'times' (multiply) and with David's you divide.

Answer $= \dfrac{7 \times 15}{5} = 21$

Once you get the hang of this, it's really quick and easy.

Proportionality questions are easy to spot because they usually include the words 'is proportional to', 'is directly proportional to' or 'varies directly with'.

Just to recap

With direct proportion:

- if one variable gets bigger then the other variable gets bigger

- if one variable gets smaller the other gets smaller.

X-Direct appears throughout this book, solving a whole range of different problems.

Answers to Questions 1–4

1 People   Arrows

74 ⟍⟋ 333

52 ⟋⟍

$\dfrac{52 \times 333}{74} = 234$

2 Percentage   People

15 ⟍⟋ 252

100 ⟋⟍

$\dfrac{252 \times 100}{15} = 1680$

3 Degrees   People

360 ⟍⟋ 300

     ⟋⟍ 80

$\dfrac{360 \times 80}{300} = 96°$

4 Chips   Nuggets

126 ⟍⟋ 4.5

350 ⟋⟍

$\dfrac{350 \times 4.5}{126} = 12.5$ nuggets

Exercise 2.1

1 A recipe for 24 blueberry muffins takes 210 grams of butter. How many muffins could you make if you use 280 grams of butter?

2 In the Last Burp Saloon, the barman served 150 customers from 27 litres of moonshine. How many people could he serve from 4.5 litres?

3 Swindler Sam trades $153.60 for 351.50 Mexican pesos. How much would he offer for 623.20 Mexican pesos?

Answers

3 $272.33
2 25
1 32

TAKE A BREAK

Take a short break before you tackle percentages.

Percentages

Percentages feature prominently throughout GCSE Maths papers, so this section may help you pick up some valuable marks!

If you have a method which works for you, then continue to use it on the questions at the end. If not, try X-Direct.

Percentages Using X-Direct

One hundred per cent, or 100%, means the whole, original or total amount.

This, unbelievably, is almost all you have to know to use this method.

Type 1 – finding a percentage of a number

Example 2.2

What is 35% of 210?

Solution

100% is the original amount of 210.

We need to find the number that is 35%.

Number   Percentage (%)

210 ⤫ 100
        35

Using X-Direct, $\dfrac{210 \times 35}{100} = 73.5$

So your answer, as it should be in the Number column, is 73.5.

Type 2 – finding one number as a percentage of another

Example 2.3

In Bodge City, 35 out of 112 people questioned owned horses. Express this as a percentage.

Solution

100% refers to the total number of people, i.e. 112.

People   Percentage (%)

112 ⤫ 100
35

Using X-Direct, $\dfrac{35 \times 100}{112} = 31.25\%$

As this answer would go in the Percentage column, the answer is 31.25% (or 31% to the nearest whole number).

Type 3 – when the figure that you are given does not refer to 100%

Example 2.4

Bodge City Bank was broken into and 5% of the amount of money stolen was offered as a reward for information. If the reward was $11 200, how much was stolen?

Solution

The original amount was 100%.

Percentage   Dollars ($)

100 ⤫
5   11 200

Using X-Direct, $\dfrac{100 \times 11\,200}{5} = \$224\,000$

Can you see that it does not matter where the gap in the table is, as long as you keep the numbers in the correct column, and the numbers that relate to each other are next to each other?

Exercise 2.2

1 Bodge City's only tycoon owned 74% of the buffalo. If there were 1600 buffalo in the city, how many did he own?

2 The Grocery Store bought beans for $350 and sold them for $448. Express the profit as a percentage of the original cost.

3 The Old Mule Express lost 6% of its post. If it lost 114 letters, how many letters was it carrying originally?

4 O'Flannery's Tannery reduced all saddles priced at $15.50 by $5.50. Express this reduction as a percentage to the nearest 0.1%.

5 Shady Deals Finance Company charged 125% interest per annum on its loans. If it lent $4000, what would be the interest charged in a year?

6 In a fight, 7.5% of the glasses in the Last Burp Saloon were smashed. If 240 were broken, how many glasses did they have originally?

Answers

1 1184 **2** 28% **3** 1900 **4** 35.5% **5** $5000 **6** 3200

Back to Olde England!

VAT questions

At the time of writing this book, VAT is 17.5%. This is a tax put on most items that you would buy in the shops. Questions on VAT are very common in exams.

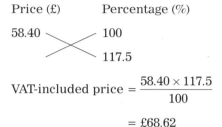

Adding on VAT

Example 2.5

The pre-VAT price of a toy is £58.40. Find the VAT-inclusive price.

Solution

Method 1 Work out 17.5% and add it to the original price.

Price (£)   Percentage (%)

58.40   100

                   17.5

$$\frac{58.40 \times 17.5}{100} = 10.22$$

VAT-inclusive price = £58.40 + £10.22

= £68.62

Method 2 Use the VAT-inclusive percentage of 117.5%.

Price (£)   Percentage (%)

58.40   100

                   117.5

$$\text{VAT-included price} = \frac{58.40 \times 117.5}{100}$$

$$= £68.62$$

Removing the VAT from the VAT-inclusive price

As you saw in the example above, the VAT-inclusive price is 100% + 17.5% = 117.5%.

If you want to find the original price, you want 100%, or if you want to find the VAT, you need the 17.5%.

Example 2.6

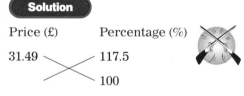

A can opener is priced at £31.49 including VAT.

Find its price before VAT was added.

Solution

Price (£)   Percentage (%)

31.49   117.5

                   100

$$\text{Pre-VAT price} = \frac{31.49 \times 100}{117.5}$$

$$= £26.80$$

Notice that the price is written as £26.80, **not** £26.8!

Example 2.7

Find the VAT charged if the price including VAT is £16.92.

Solution

Price (£)   Percentage (%)

16.92   117.5

                 17.5

$$\text{VAT} = \frac{16.92 \times 17.5}{117.5} = £2.52$$

Exercise 2.3

1 A toy is priced at £57.34 including VAT. Find its price excluding VAT.

2 If the VAT on a computer is £218.75, what is its price including VAT?

3 A CD is priced at £16.45 including VAT. In a sale, Chears Ltd. offers 17% off this price, while Rock & Soul Records offer it at the exclusive of VAT price. Which company offers the better deal?

Chears offer the better deal.
3 Chears £13.65, Rock and Soul £14.00
2 £1468.75
1 £48.80

Answers

Exponential growth and decay

AP^T amount × percentage^{time}

In this formula, 'percentage' means the new percentage with which you have to calculate (i.e. when adding 5%, write 1.05, when adding 17% write 1.17, subtracting 3% write 0.97, subtracting 15% write 0.85).

Example 2.8

Prospecting Pat invests $650 at 5% for 7 years in the Bodge City Bank. Find the total at the end of this period.

Solution

$$AP^T = 650 \times 1.05^7 = \$914.62$$

Example 2.9

Wealth Valley's population of 18 000 decreases at the rate of 3 per cent per annum (i.e. per year) for 6 years. Find the total population at the end of this period.

Solution

$$AP^T = 18\,000 \times 0.97^6 = 14\,993 \text{ to the nearest person}$$

Exercise 2.4

1 The area of farmland in Aridzona grew by 4% per annum for 10 years. If it was 1400 acres initially, find the area of farmland at the end of the period.

2 After the gold rush in 1860, the citizens of Kanvas City left at the annual rate of 3.5%. What was the population after 20 years if it was 11 400 during the gold rush? Give your answer to the nearest 100 people.

2 5600 people
1 2072 acres

Answers

Do not use the EXP or EE button on your calculator when you are doing exponential questions.

TAKE A BREAK

you deserve one!

19

Variation

$y \propto x$ means y is proportional to x

$y \propto x^2$ means y is proportional to x^2

$y \propto \dfrac{1}{x}$ means y is inversely proportional to x

$y \propto \dfrac{1}{x^2}$ means y is inversely proportional to x^2

Replace 'proportional to' with '$= k$'.

In 'inversely', change the i to a 1 and the n to an o, then the first five letters give '1 over'.

Thus $y \propto x$ becomes $y = kx$

$y \propto \dfrac{1}{x^2}$ becomes $y = k \times \dfrac{1}{x^2}$ or $y = \dfrac{k}{x^2}$

In questions like these you have to find the constant k using values given for x and y. Then the question will give another value for x or y and you will have to find the missing variable using the value of k that you have calculated.

Example 2.10

y is proportional to x^3. When $x = 1.6$, $y = 17.2$. Find:

a) y when $x = 0.6$

b) x when $y = 196$.

Solution

$y \propto x^3$

First find the value of k using the given x and y values.

$y = kx^3$

$17.2 = k(1.6)^3$

$17.2 = 4.096k$

$k = \dfrac{17.2}{4.096}$

$\quad = 4.2$ correct to 1 d.p.

a) When $x = 0.6 \quad y = 4.2x^3$

$\qquad = 4.2 \times 0.6^3$

$\qquad = 0.91$ correct to 2 d.p.

b) When $y = 196 \quad y = 4.2x^3$

$\qquad 196 = 4.2x^3$

$\qquad \dfrac{196}{4.2} = x^3$

$\qquad x = \sqrt[3]{\dfrac{196}{4.2}}$

$\qquad = 3.6$ correct to 1 d.p.

Remember that the inverse, or opposite, of cubing is cube rooting or working to the power of $\frac{1}{3}$.

Example 2.11

y is inversely proportional to x^2 and $x = 0.162$ when $y = 471$. Find:

a) y when $x = 1.34$

b) x when $y = 302$

giving all answers correct to three significant figures.

Solution

Firstly, find k.

$y \propto \dfrac{1}{x^2}$

So $y = \dfrac{k}{x^2}$

$471 = \dfrac{k}{(0.162)^2}$

$k = 471 \times (0.162)^2$

$\quad = 12.36$

To minimise later rounding errors, either use the calculator memory for k or round it to four or five significant figures.

a) When $x = 1.34$

$$y = \frac{k}{x^2}$$

$$y = \frac{12.36}{1.34^2}$$

$$= 6.88 \text{ correct to 3 s.f.}$$

b) When $y = 302$

$$302 = \frac{12.36}{x^2}$$

$$302x^2 = 12.36$$

$$x^2 = \frac{12.36}{302} = 0.040\ 93$$

$$x = 0.202 \text{ correct to 3 s.f.}$$

Exercise 2.5

1 y is proportional to x^2. If $y = 21.3$ when $x = 7.2$, find:
a) the value of y when $x = 1.7$
b) the value of x when $y = 41.3$.

2 y is inversely proportional to x^3. If $y = 141.1$ when $x = 1.45$, find:
a) y when $x = 2.74$
b) x when $y = 444.3$.

3 y varies directly as the cube root of x. If $y = 3.44$ when $x = 71.2$, find:
a) y when $x = 106.8$
b) x when $y = 4.75$.

4 y varies inversely with the square root of x. If $y = 32.1$ when $x = 43.2$, find:
a) y when $x = 55.7$
b) x when $y = 20.1$.

Answers

1 $k = 0.41$ **a)** $y = 1.2$ **b)** $x = 10.0$
2 $k = 430.2$ **a)** $y = 20.9$ **b)** $x = 0.99$
3 $k = 0.83$ **a)** $y = 3.94$ **b)** $x = 187.5$
4 $k = 211$ **a)** $y = 28.3$ **b)** $x = 110.2$

Simplification of ratios

Ratios can be simplified by using X-Direct.

Example 2.12

Write $5 : 4$ in the ratio:

a) $1 : k$ **b)** $k : 1$.

Solution

a)
```
5       4
 \     /
  \   /
   \ /
    X
   / \
  /   \
 /     \
1
```

$$k = \frac{1 \times 4}{5} = 0.8$$

b)
```
5       4
 \     /
  \   /
   \ /
    X
   / \
  /   \
 /     \
        1
```

$$k = \frac{5 \times 1}{4} = 1.25$$

Exercise 2.6

1 Pot-bellied Pete shares his blueberry muffins with his mate Skinny-ribbed Sam in the ratio $7 : 2$. If his bag contains 36 muffins, how many muffins does each receive? What fraction of the original does Skinny-ribbed Sam receive?

2 Write the ratio $12 : 5$ in the form

a) $n : 1$ **b)** $1 : n$.

Answers

1 Pete gets 28, Sam gets 8; $\frac{2}{9}$
2 a) $2.4 : 1$ **b)** $1 : 0.42$

TAKE A BREAK

Before you tackle the exam questions take a break and update your mind maps. Have you started an X-Direct mind map yet? If not, this would be a good time to try.

Time to bite the bullet!

Exam-type questions 2

1 Doc Hogmanay buys a painting of his dear old grannie for £11 200 and sells it for £13 550. Find his percentage profit based on the original price.

2 362 drachmas = 2820 lire.
   a) How many lire can you get for 1584 drachmas?
   b) How many drachmas can be exchanged for 50 605 lire?

3 A car goes 18.6 km on 4.4 litres of fuel.
   a) How far does it go on 20 litres?
   b) How many litres would it use to go 100 km?
   Write both answers correct to 3 sig. figs.

4 The VAT added to the price of an article is £5.67. What was the pre-VAT price of the article?

5 The diagram shows the composition of the membership of a Sports Club.

	Under 25	Over 25
Men	36	54
Women	24	36

Calculate in its simplest form, the ratio of:
   a) male to female
   b) under 25s to over 25s.

6 Express the ratio 5 : 2 in the form:
   a) $n : 1$
   b) $1 : n$.

7 A car is bought for £9250 and sold the following year for £7800. Express the depreciation in value as a percentage of the cost price.

8 A prize of £450 is divided among Arrow-biting Andy, Bootlegging Bob and Cowpoking Clint in the ratio 6 : 7 : 2. How much does each receive?

9 y varies directly as x^2 and $y = 72.4$ when $x = 5.1$.
   a) Find y when $x = 2.8$.
   b) Find x when $y = 104.2$.
   Give both answers correct to 1 d.p.

10 y is inversely proportional to $\sqrt{x}$ and $y = 3.8$ when $x = 0.17$.
   a) Find y when $x = 0.57$.
   b) Find x when $y = 8.7$.

11 Wages of £72 are shared between Aridzona Alice, Beat'm Up Betty and Crazy-horse Carol, so that Alice receives $\frac{1}{2}$ of the money, Betty receives $\frac{2}{3}$ of the remainder and Carol receives the amount left. Find:
   a) the amount Betty receives
   b) the fraction remaining for Carol.

12 The manager of a function hall calculates the charge per person using the formula:
$$C = \frac{k\sqrt{T}}{n}$$
where T is the number of hours booked, n is the number of people attending and k is a constant.
   a) Find k if the cost per person was £2.40 when the hall was booked for 4 hours for a function attended by 80 people.
   b) Find the cost per person for a function for 24 people which lasted 9 hours.
   c) Rewrite the formula in the form $C = kT^x n^y$ stating the values of x and y.

Answers

1 21%
2 a) 12 339 lira   **b)** 6496 drachma
3 a) 84.5 km   **b)** 23.7 litres
4 £32.40
5 a) 3 : 2   **b)** 2 : 3
6 2.5 : 1 and 1 : 0.4
7 16%
8 £180, £210, £60
9 $k = 72.4 \div 5.1^2 = 2.784$
   a) 21.8   **b)** $\sqrt{104.2 \div 2.784} = 6.1$
10 $k = 3.8 \times \sqrt{0.17} = 1.57$
   a) 2.1   **b)** 0.03
11 a) £24   **b)** $\frac{1}{6}$
12 a) 96   **b)** £12.00   **c)** $x = \frac{1}{2}, y = -1$

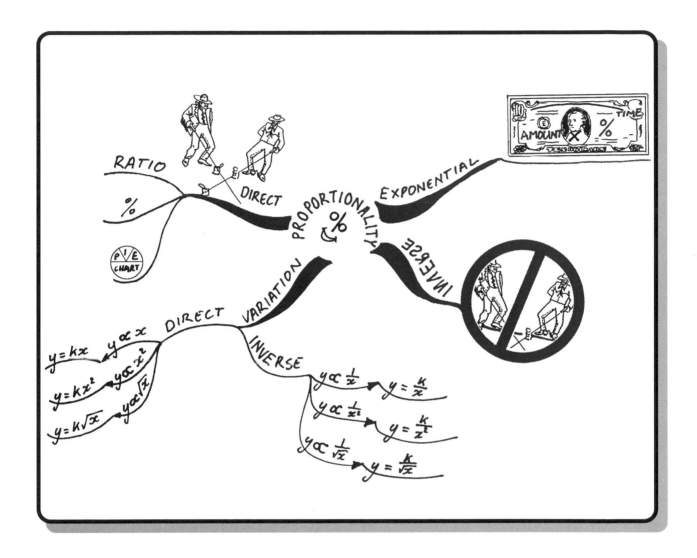

2

review

How much have you learnt?

Tick off each topic in the list when you are confident you can cope with it.

- Answer questions on ratio and proportion.
- Work out a percentage of a number.
- Express one number as a percentage of another.
- Solve problems involving VAT.
- Work out problems involving exponential growth or decay.
- Find constants of proportionality in questions on variation.
- Simplify ratios.

Graphs

preview

By the end of this chapter you will be able to:

- **identify the gradient and y-intercept from the equation of a straight line**

- **draw a tangent to a curve at a given point**

- **find the area under a graph**

- **identify what the area under a graph represents**

- **solve simultaneous equations graphically**

- **sketch quadratic equations**

- **convert a non-linear graph to a linear graph by changing variables**

- **find values of the constants in a non-linear function**

- **transform functions**

- **draw trigonometric graphs**

- **find the values of an unknown, in a given range, that satisfy a trigonometric equation**

- **solve problems using linear programming**

- **find a range of values that satisfy an algebraic inequality**

- **maximise or minimise an expression**

- **recognise graphs of mathematical equations**

Straight-line graphs

Straight-line graphs have equations or formulae of the form:

$$y = mx + c \quad \text{or} \quad ax + by = c.$$

Gradient and y-intercept

There are two alternative ways of tackling questions involving straight-line graphs. You may need either approach.

1 – the algebraic method

If your equation is not in the form $y = mx + c$, then rearrange it so that it is.

m gives the gradient

c gives the y-intercept

For example, if the equation is $y = 2x - 1$, the gradient = 2, the y-intercept = –1.

If the equation is $2y + x = 2$, rearrange it to get y on its own.

$$2y = 2 - x$$

Halving all terms gives:

$$y = 1 - \tfrac{1}{2}x$$

$$\text{gradient} = -\tfrac{1}{2}$$

$$y\text{-intercept} = 1$$

2 – tabulation

Draw up a table inserting sensible values for x. Sometimes you may be able to use a short cut, especially for equations of the form $ax + by = c$.

For example, if the equation is $2x + 5y = 20$, substitute $x = 0$ to give $y = 4$, and substitute $y = 0$ to give $x = 10$.

Plot the points (0, 4) and (10, 0) and join them up.

It is always wise to check by finding a third point and making sure it is on the line you have drawn.

Tangent to a curve

Example 3.1

Find the gradient of the given curve at the point (2, 6).

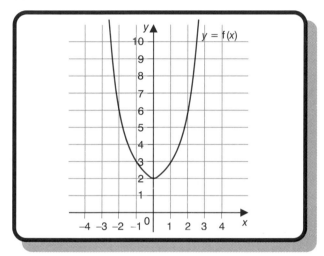

Solution

Draw a tangent to the curve at the given point. Choose two points along the tangent, and work out the gradient by using

Gradients are GROTty
(Gradient = Rise Over Tread) or
Gradients are GRADUAL (GRADient = Up/ALong)
or your own method.

From the diagrams: gradient $= \dfrac{8}{2} = 4$

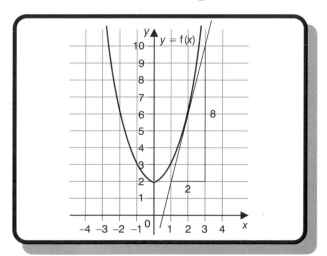

The meaning of the gradient

The gradient means the measure on the y-axis divided by that on the x-axis. Alternatively, it means y per x. For example, on a distance-time graph, the gradient gives the speed. On a speed-time graph it gives the acceleration.

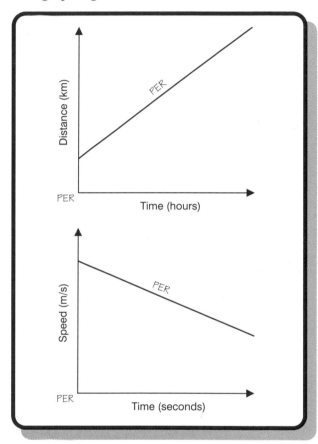

Area under a graph

On a straight-line graph:

- y-units divided by x-units gives the gradient

- y-units multiplied by x-units gives the area.

For example, on a speed-time graph:

- the speed (y-unit, m/s) divided by the time (x-unit, s) gives the acceleration (m/s^2)

- the area under the graph (speed in m/s times time in s) gives the distance travelled.

The question will probably ask you to find the area under a graph either by counting squares or by using the trapezium rule.

3

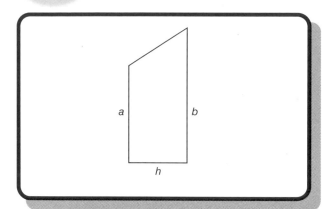

Area of a trapezium = $\frac{1}{2}(a + b)h$

This is usually given on the *Information and formulae* sheet.

Example 3.2

Use the trapezium rule to find the area under the graph below.

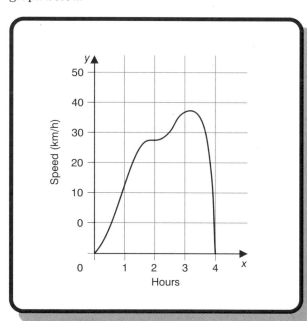

Solution

Area = $\frac{1}{2}(0 + 12) \times 1 + \frac{1}{2}(12 + 28) \times 1$

$+ \frac{1}{2}(28 + 36) \times 1 + \frac{1}{2}(36 + 0) \times 1$

= 76 km

Exercise 3.1

1 Pot-bellied Pete falls asleep in the bath. Water spills over the side as indicated in the diagram below.

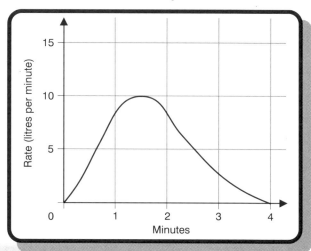

a) Find the gradient at 2 minutes.
b) Find the area under the curve.
c) What does this area represent?

2 This is a speed-time graph for a journey made by the Transaridzona Express between Bodge City and Kanvas City.

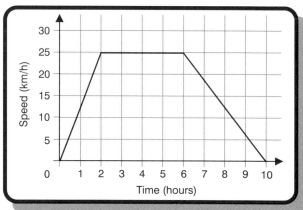

a) What is the initial rate of acceleration of the train?
b) What is the final rate of deceleration of the train?
c) What is the distance between the two towns?
State the units used in all answers.

Answers

2 a) 12.5 km/h² **b)** 6.25 km/h² **c)** 175 km
1 a) between −6.5 and −7 **b)** about 20 **c)** volume of water (in litres) spilt in 4 minutes

Simultaneous equations

Graphical solution

When you are asked to solve simultaneous equations, the graphs of the equations will be given to you and the coordinates of the point(s) where they cross (or intersect) will give the solution(s) for x and y.

Example 3.3

Using graph paper, draw accurately the graphs for the following equations.

$x + 2y = 7$

$x - y = 4$

Hence solve these two simultaneous equations graphically.

Solution

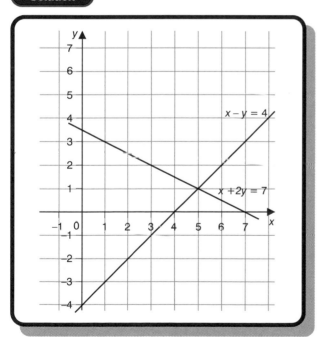

The lines cross at (5, 1), so the solution is $x = 5$, $y = 1$.

Example 3.4

By drawing suitable lines on the graph $y = 2x^2 - x$ below, solve the following equations.

a) $2x^2 - x = x + 2$ **b)** $2x^2 - x - 5 = 0$

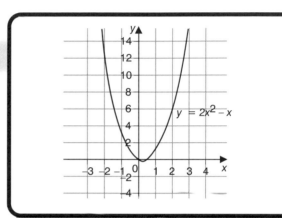

Solution

a) Draw $y = x + 2$ on the graph.

The lines cross when $x = 1.6$ and -0.6 so the solution of the equation $2x^2 - x = x + 2$ is $x = 1.6, -0.6$.

b) Rearrange the equation so that $2x^2 - x$ is on one side. This gives $2x^2 - x = 5$. Now draw the line $y = 5$.

The lines cross when $x = -1.35$ and 1.85 so the solution is $x = -1.35, 1.85$.

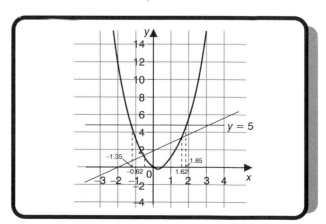

Solution of quadratic equations – sketching quadratic equations

- Quadratic equations are symmetrical.

- They have either a minimum or a maximum point.

- They cross the x-axis a maximum of twice.

- Solving a quadratic equation gives the x-values of the points where the curve crosses the x-axis.

Example 3.5

Solve the equation $x^2 - 5x + 5 = 0$ graphically.

Solution

Tabulate the values as follows.

x		−2	−1	0	1	2	3	4	5
$y = x^2 - 5x + 5$		19	11	5	1	−1	−1	1	5

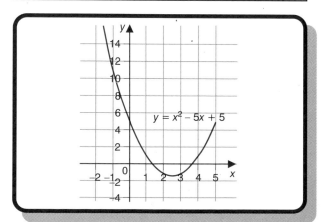

The curve $y = x^2 - 5x + 5$ crosses the $y = 0$ line (or x-axis) at $x = 1.4$ and $x = 3.6$. These are the roots of the equation $x^2 - 5x + 5 = 0$.

Converting a non-linear graph to a linear graph by changing axes

This is a method of making an equation that would normally be a curve into a straight line. For example, look at the equation $q = ap^2 + b$ and compare it to

$Y = MX + C$ (the usual equation of a straight line).

The equation is shown in capitals to avoid confusion in case a question gives a relationship of the form $y = ax^2 + b$.

On the X-axis plot values of p^2.

On the Y-axis plot values of q.

When q is plotted against p^2 the points should be on, or nearly on, a straight line.

Drawing the line of best fit gives:

M, the gradient which is a

C, the y-intercept which is b.

Example 3.6

The table of values below shows how s and t are related.

s	0.6	1.3	1.8	2.5	3.1
t	2.7	3.6	4.7	6.8	9.1

Plot the values of t against s^2 on a suitable graph.

It is believed that t is related to s by the equation $t = as^2 + b$.

a) Explain how the graph confirms this relationship.

b) Estimate values for a and b correct to 1 d.p., and hence state the relationship between s and t.

Solution

1 On the axes below, draw the graphs of $y = x^3$ and $y = 25 - 6x$. From your graphs, estimate a solution to the equation $x^3 + 6x - 25 = 0$.

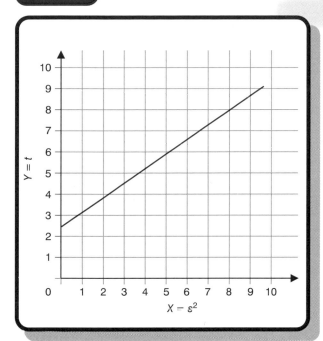

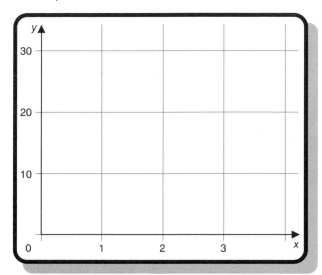

a) The graph is a straight line of the form
$y = mx + c$.

b) a = the gradient = 0.7

b = y-intercept = 2.4

Therefore, the final equation is $t = 0.7s^2 + 2.4$.

2 Using the axes below, draw the graph of
$y = x^2 - 4x + 2$.
  a) From your graph, estimate the solutions of
  $x^2 - 4x = -2$.
  b) By drawing a suitable line, find approximate values of
  x for which $x^2 - 4x + 2 = x + 3$.

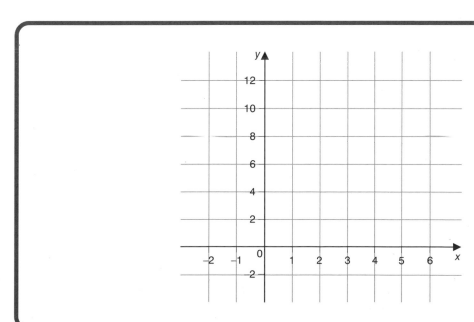

3 Two variables are related by the equation $q = a\sqrt{p} + k$, where a and k are constants.

p	5.4	18.1	41.2	60.1	96.7
q	7.5	6.6	5.5	4.8	3.8

By plotting q against $\sqrt{p}$, draw a line of best fit and hence estimate the values of a and k correct to 1 d.p.

TAKE A BREAK

Now is a good time to take a break and think back over what you have done so far.

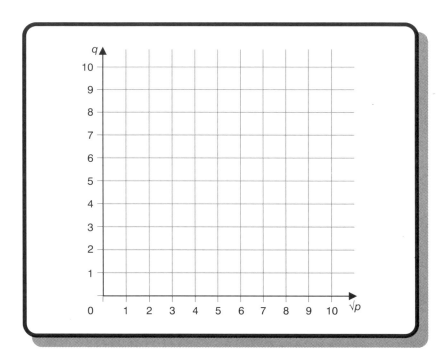

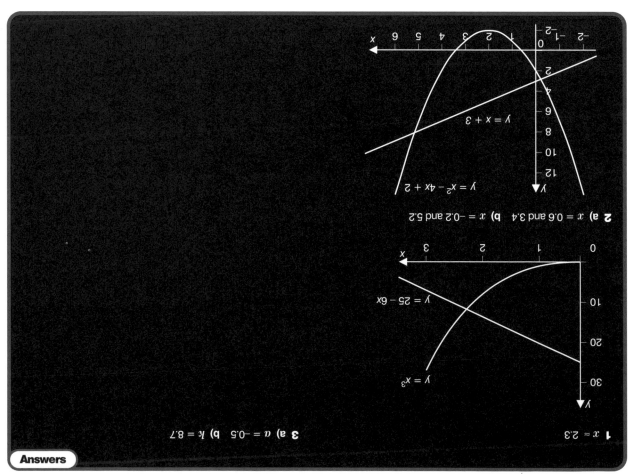

Answers

1 $x \approx 2.3$

2 a) $x = 0.6$ and 3.4 **b)** $x = -0.2$ and 5.2

$y = x + 3$

$y = x^2 - 4x + 2$

$y = 25 - 6x$

$y = x^3$

3 a) $a = -0.5$ **b)** $k = 8.7$

Finding the values of the constants in a non-linear equation

Example 3.7

Variables y and x are related by the equation $y = ab^x$. The graph below shows the relationship. Using this graph, estimate the values of a and b.

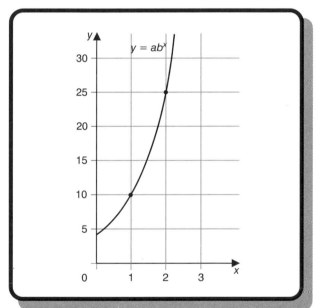

Solution

Substituting $x = 0$ gives $y = ab^0 = a$ (because any number to the power of zero is 1).

So $(0, 4)$ gives the value of a as 4.

When $x = 1$, $y = ab$.

As $y = 10$ when $x = 1$, we find $b = 2.5$.

Functions

A relation between two variables, x and y, can be written as $y = f(x)$.

$f(x + c)$ moves $f(x)$ c units to the left.

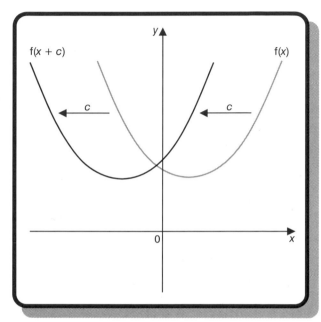

$f(x - c)$ moves $f(x)$ c units to the right.

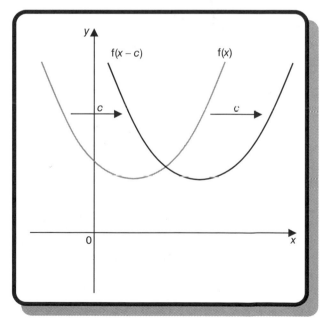

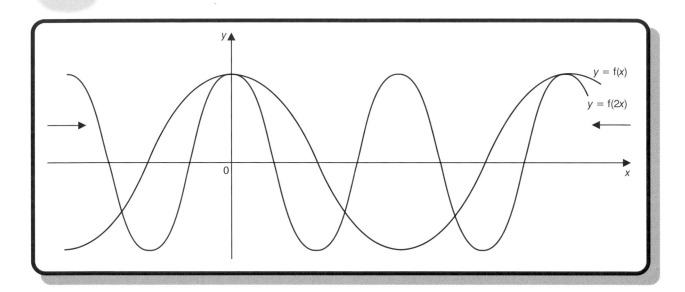

With f($2x$), the Last Burp Saloon's accordionist, Con Seteenar squashes f(x) towards the y-axis to half its width.

With f($\frac{1}{2}x$), he stretches it to twice its width.

Summary for movements in the x-direction!

Putting a number with the x inside the f(x) can make you cross!

It goes the opposite way to what you would expect.

Adding to x moves the line of f(x) to the left.

Subtracting from x moves the line of f(x) to the right.

Multiplying by a number greater than 1 squashes the line of f(x) towards the y-axis.

Dividing by a number greater than 1 (or multiplying by a fraction) stretches f(x) from the y-axis.

However, adding, subtracting, multiplying or dividing outside the f(x) moves the graph in the positive or negative vertical direction as you would expect.

Adding to f(x) moves f(x) upwards.

Subtracting from f(x) moves f(x) downwards.

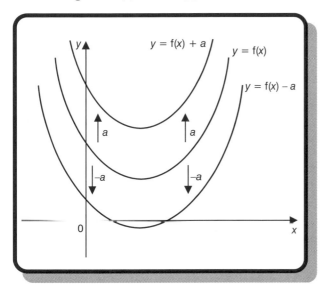

Multiplying f(x) by a whole number stretches f(x) from the x-axis.

Dividing f(x) by a whole number (or multiplying by a fraction) squashes f(x) towards the x-axis.

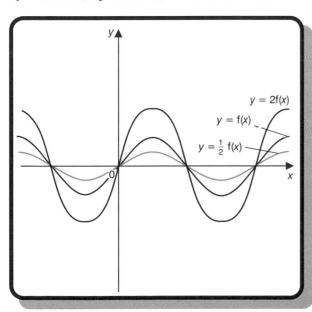

Exercise 3.3

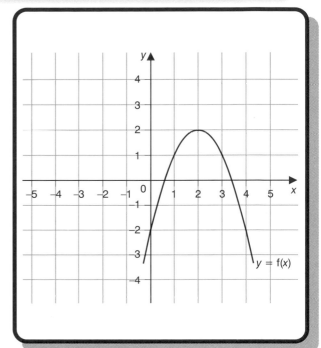

The graph above illustrates $y = $ f(x). On the same axes sketch:

1 $y = $ f($x + 5$)

2 $y = $ f($2x$)

3 $y = 2$f(x)

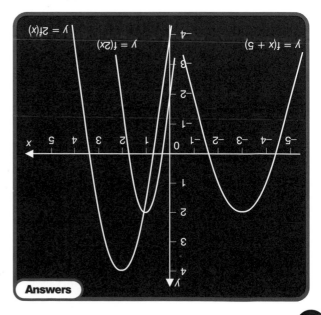

Answers

35

3

Sin, cos and tan graphs

Sine and cosine graphs have the same basic shape. The sine graph starts from the origin (remember original sin), but the cosine graph starts from 1 on the y-axis when $x = 0$ (the cos1ne graph).

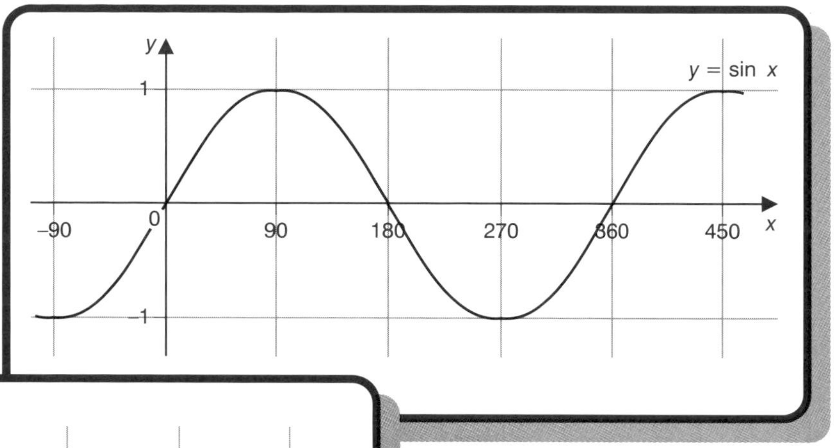

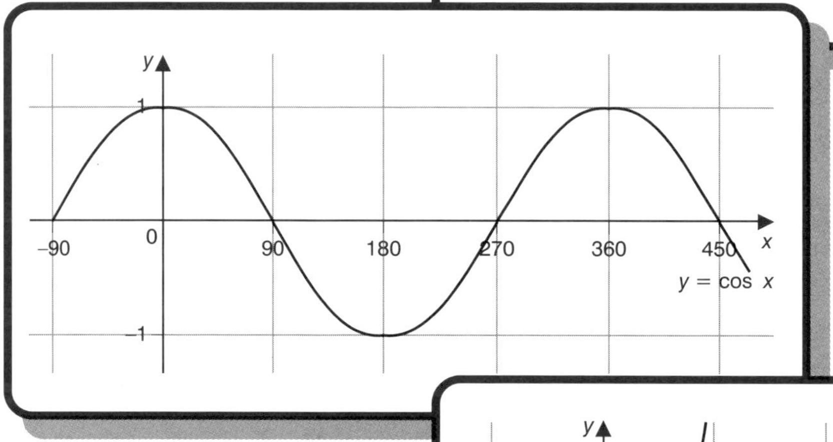

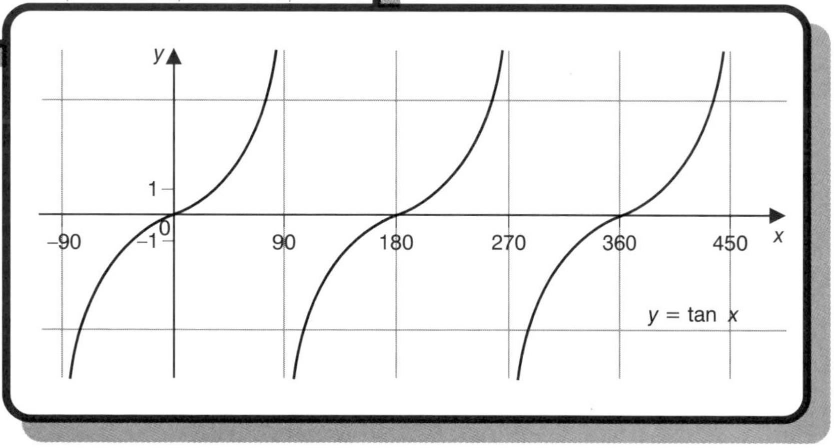

$y = \sin x$

$y = \cos x$

Tan is completely different, but perhaps Dr Tan's Baked Beans (which repeat every 180°) will help.

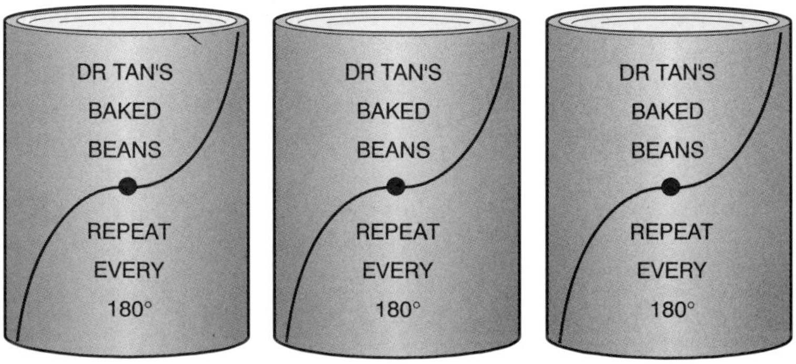

$y = \tan x$

DR TAN'S BAKED BEANS

REPEAT EVERY 180°

DR TAN'S BAKED BEANS

REPEAT EVERY 180°

DR TAN'S BAKED BEANS

REPEAT EVERY 180°

Example 3.8

Find the solutions for x in the range $0° \leqslant x < 360°$, which satisfy these equations.

a) $\sin x = 0.5$ b) $\cos x = 0.5$

c) $\cos x = 0.61$ d) $\tan x = -0.2$

Solution

a) Draw the graph of $y = \sin x$, then draw a horizontal dotted line for $y = 0.5$. This crosses the $y = \sin x$ graph at two places. The solutions are where the line cuts the graph. Using your calculator for inverse sin (0.5) will give you one solution i.e. 30°. The other solution is found from the graph. It is $180° - 30°$ (or $90° + 60°$) at 150°.

The solutions are $x = 30°, 150°$.

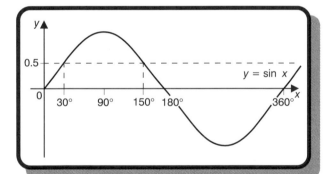

b) Draw the graph of $y = \cos x$, then draw a horizontal dotted line for $y = 0.5$.

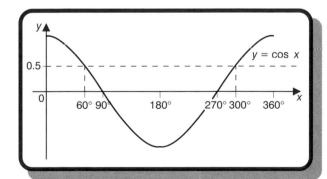

This crosses the $y = \cos x$ graph at two places, giving the two solutions.

Using your calculator for inverse cos (0.5) will give you one solution i.e. 60°. The other is the same distance from 360° so it is $360° - 60° = 300°$.

The solutions are $x = 60°, 300°$.

c) Again, draw the graph of $y = \cos x$ and add a line at $y = 0.61$. The solutions are where the line cuts the graph. Your calculator will give you inverse cos (0.61) = 52.4°. The other solution is at $360° - 52.4°$ (or $270° + 37.6°$).

The solutions are $x = 52.4°, 307.6°$.

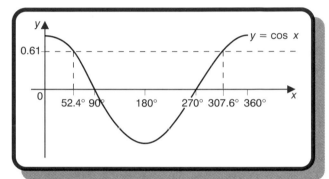

d) Draw the graph of $y = \tan x$ and then draw a horizontal dotted line for $y = -0.2$. Where this line crosses the $y = \tan x$ graph gives the solutions.

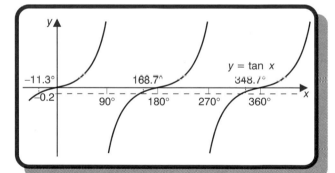

Using your calculator for inverse tan (-0.2) will give you $-11.3°$. This is a negative solution, and you want solutions between 0° and 360°. Don't despair, just ask Dr Tan! Add 180° to $-11.3°$ to get 168.7°, then add 180° again to find the second solution.

The solutions are $x = 168.7°, 348.7°$.

3

You may have solved questions like these using the CAST diagram. If you are more at home with this method, stick with it.

S	A
T	C

Remember that you nearly always get more than one solution for this type of question.

Exercise 3.4

Sketch the sin, cos and tan graphs, then find all the solutions for x, correct to one decimal place, in the range $0° \leq x < 360°$ for the following equations.

1 $\sin x = 0.89$

2 $\tan x = -0.41$

3 $\cos x = 0.24$

4 $\sin x = -0.12$

5 $\cos x = 0.91$

6 $\tan x = \sqrt{3}$

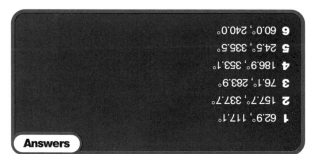

Answers

6 $60.0°, 240.0°$

5 $24.5°, 335.5°$

4 $186.9°, 353.1°$

3 $76.1°, 283.9°$

2 $157.7°, 337.7°$

1 $62.9°, 117.1°$

TAKE A BREAK

All things being equal, this is a good time to take a break. Inequalities are next on the menu.

Linear programming

The three skills you need for these questions are:

- converting the information given into algebraic inequalities

- drawing lines for the inequalities

- choosing the region.

Some questions also ask for an expression to be maximised or minimised.

Converting information into algebraic inequalities

There are always two variables. Questions are often confusing. For example:

- *'no more than' or 'at most' means 'less than or equal to'*

- *'no less than' or 'at least' means 'more than or equal to'*

Make sure the multiple is on the correct side.

For instance, in algebra 'y is twice the size of x' becomes $y = 2x$, so 'y is at least twice the size of x' would be $y \geq 2x$.

Example 3.9

In the following inequalities, x represents the number of men and y represents the number of women.

Write inequalities for each of these.

a) A stadium will seat at most 20 000 people.

b) There must be at least 500 men and no more than 15 000 women.

c) On average, the men weigh 110 kg and the women weigh 55 kg. A lift can hold at most 1100 kg.

d) There should be not more than twice as many men as women.

Solution

a) $x + y \leqslant 20\,000$

b) $x \geqslant 500$ and $y \leqslant 15\,000$

c) $110x + 55y \leqslant 1100$

$\quad\quad 2x + y \leqslant 20$

(by cancelling through by 5 and 11 or 55)

d) $x \leqslant 2y$

(The question could be expressed as, 'The number of men is no more than twice the number of women.'.)

Choosing the region

You can either substitute a point in the region on either side of the line, and see if it fits the required inequality, or for positive coefficients of y, use B≤LOW and A≥OVE.

Example 3.10

The diagram below shows the graphs of $x = 1$, $y = x$, $y = 5 - x$ and $2x + y = 10$.

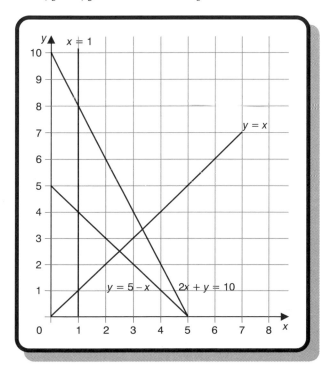

Leave unshaded the region which satisfies the following inequalities.

$x \geqslant 1$

$y \leqslant x$

$y \geqslant 5 - x$

$2x + y \leqslant 10$

Solution

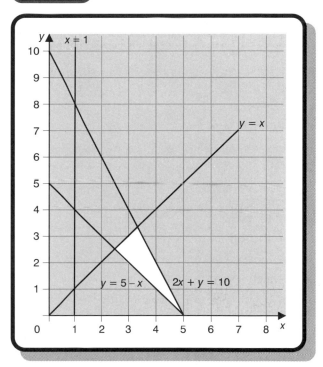

In the above inequalities, the coefficient of y is positive. Therefore:

$y \leqslant x$ is represented by the region vertically B≤LOW the line $y = x$.

$y \geqslant 5 - x$ is represented by the region A≥OVE $y = 5 - x$.

$2x + y \leqslant 10$ is represented by the region vertically B≤LOW $2x + y = 10$.

*Usually the questions ask you to leave the required area **unshaded**, but occasionally they request the required region to be **shaded**.*

39

Maximising or minimising an expression

The required values are either at or as near as possible to a vertex of the wanted region. The points to be included must usually take whole-number values within the region. It often helps to convert the information which is to be maximised or minimised into an algebraic expression.

Example 3.11

Suppose you are set a question concerning the numbers of adults (x) and children (y) attending a rodeo, and you are asked to find the maximum profit, subject to certain inequalities.

If the profit on every adult ticket is $5 and on each child is $3, give an expression for the profit made. Hence find the maximum profit.

Solution

Profit $= 5x + 3y$

The maximum profit is found by substituting the coordinates at or nearest to the vertices of the wanted region into this expression, and finding which gives the maximum profit.

Example 3.12

The Havago War Tribe Council can have at most 20 members. Let x represent the number of men and y the number of women. Meetings are cancelled unless at least five men are present. The Havago is an unusual tribe because there must be at least twice as many women as men present.

a) Find three inequalities that state the above information.

b) Show these inequalities on a graph, leaving the required region unshaded.

Solution

a) $x + y \leqslant 20$ $x \geqslant 5$ $y \geqslant 2x$ or $2x \leqslant y$

b)

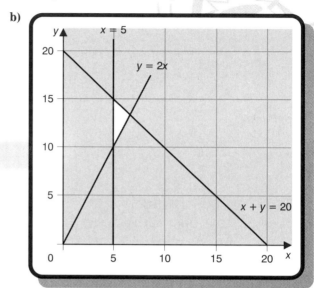

Example 3.13

Dr Tan can carry a maximum of 40 kg of baked beans. Large cans weigh 1 kg and small cans weigh half as much. (This information is already represented on the graph as the line $2x + y = 40$ where x is the number of large cans and y is the number of small cans.)

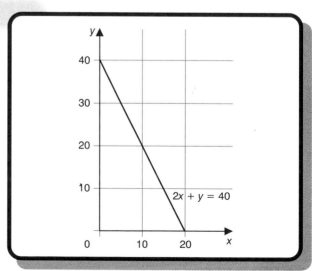

To conform with Bodge City legislation, he cannot carry more than 15 large tins. He must carry no more than twice the number of small tins as large tins.

a) Represent this information on the graph, leaving the required area unshaded.

b) If he makes $3 profit on every large tin and $2 on every small tin, what is his maximum profit?

Solution

a)

y
40 — $x = 15$ $y = 2x$
30
20
10   $2x + y = 40$
0   10   20 x

b) The expression for the profit is $P = 3x + 2y$.

The point (10, 20) gives $70 profit and at (15, 10) the profit is $65.

The answer is therefore (10, 20).

Exercise 3.5

1 Chief Sitting Duck trades horses. He can buy up to 13 horses, but has no more than $2400 to spend. Let the number of mares be x and of stallions y. Each mare costs $240 and each stallion costs $120. He must have at least five mares and five stallions. If he makes a profit of $30 per mare and $20 per stallion, how many of each should he buy to obtain the most profit?

2 Hardup Hank wants to go west with his enormous family. He can hire small or large wagons. Let the number of small wagons be x and of large wagons be y. Each small wagon can hold 8 people, and each large wagon can hold 16 people. He has to carry at least 48 people, and must have at least one of each type of wagon. Find his cheapest option if the cost is $70 for a small wagon and $100 for a large wagon.

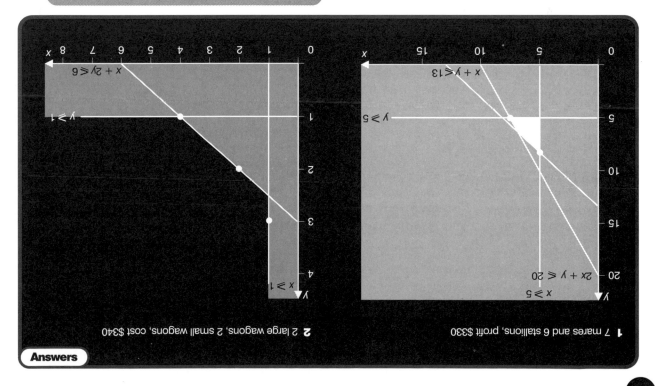

Answers

1 7 mares and 6 stallions, profit $330

2 2 large wagons, 2 small wagons, cost $340

Graphs from practical situations

These are most easily solved by describing in words what happens in reality and comparing your description to the graphs given.

Example 3.14

Water is poured into vases **(a)**, **(b)** and **(c)** at a constant rate. The graphs below show the depth of water in the vases against the time. Match each container with its graph.

Solution

Look at the vases and describe in words the speed at which the height rises.

a) Slowing down then increasing, therefore graph **(iv)**

b) Increasing, therefore graph **(iii)**

c) Constant rate, therefore **(ii)**

Example 3.15

Draw a vase which would fill up at the rate described in graph **(v)** below.

Solution

The height rises at a decreasing speed. This is an upside-down version of vase **(b)**.

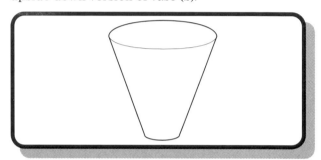

Note: If the area of the cross-section is increasing, the rate at which the depth of liquid rises is decreasing, and vice versa.

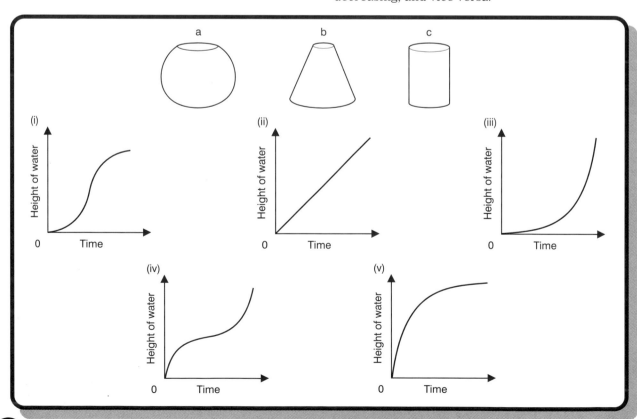

Recognising graphs of mathematical equations

The mind map below summarises the graphs you need to know.

TAKE A BREAK

Time for another break. How are the mind maps coming along?

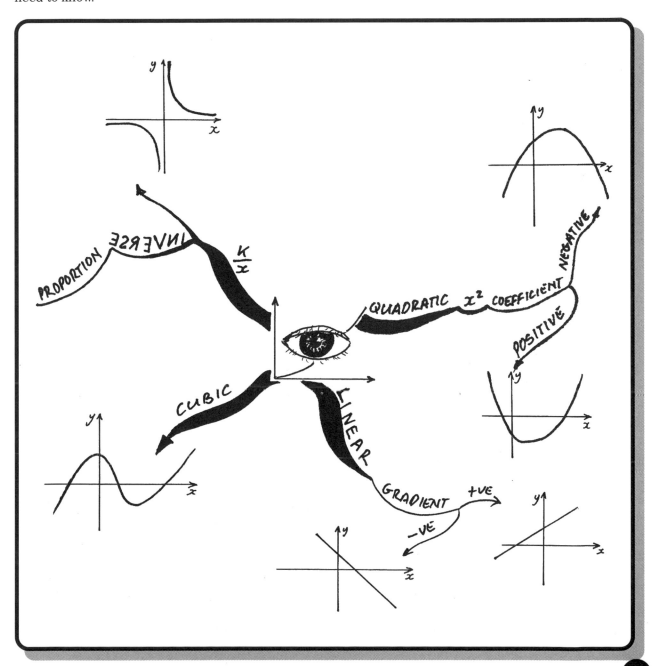

A person's gotta do what a person's gotta do!

Exam-type questions 3

1 Bacteria were placed in a culture and left to grow. A cell count was taken every hour for 9 hours. The results are as shown on the graph below.

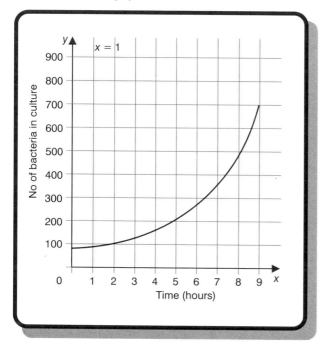

a) Draw the tangent to the curve where $t = 6$.
b) Find the gradient to the curve at this point and state its units.
c) What does this gradient represent?

2 On graph paper, draw two axes in the ranges $-2 \leqslant x \leqslant 6$, and $-4 \leqslant y \leqslant 4$. By a graphical method, solve the following simultaneous equations.
$x + y = 2$
$y = 2x - 10$

3 Study the graphs shown on the right. Which graphs could represent the following equations?
a) $x + y = 10$
b) $y = \dfrac{5}{x}$
c) $y = 10 + 9x - x^2$
d) $y = x^2$

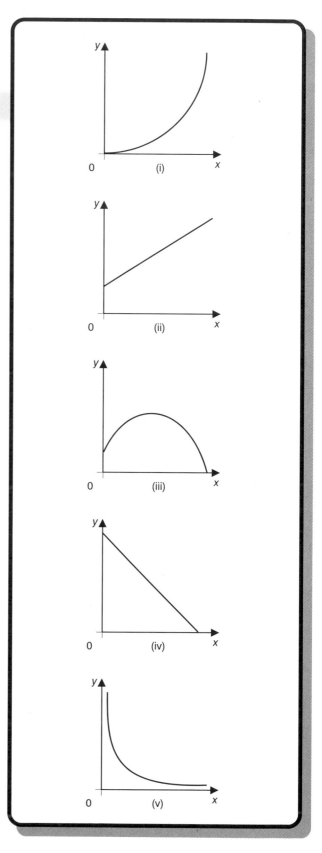

4 The diagram below shows the graph of $y = \mathrm{f}(x)$.

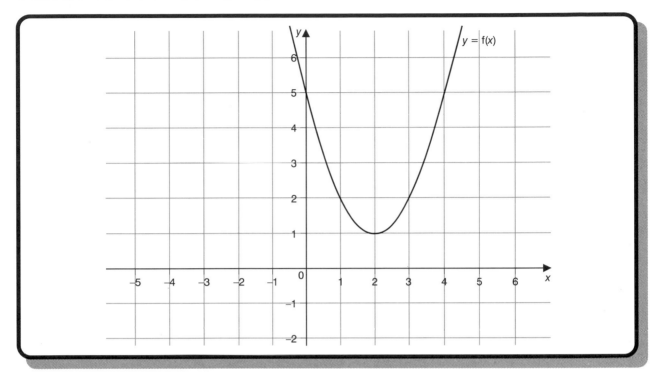

On the same graph, sketch the following functions.

a) $y = \mathrm{f}(x + 4)$ **b)** $y = \mathrm{f}(2x)$ **c)** $y = \mathrm{f}(x) - 3$

5 a) By adding a suitable construction line to the graph of $y = -\dfrac{1}{x}$ shown below, solve the equation $-\dfrac{1}{x} = 1 - x$.

b) Show that the points of intersection of the two curves are the roots of the equation $x^2 - x - 1 = 0$.

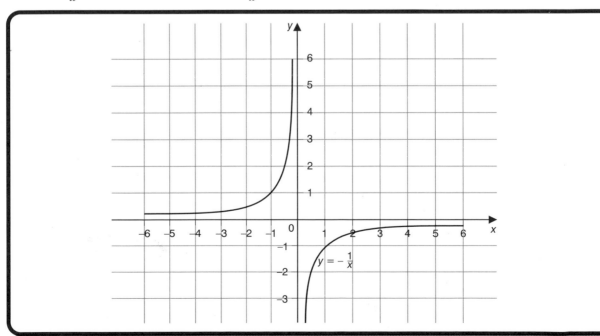

6 Estimate the distance covered in the journey shown in the speed-time graph illustrated below. State the units of measurement.

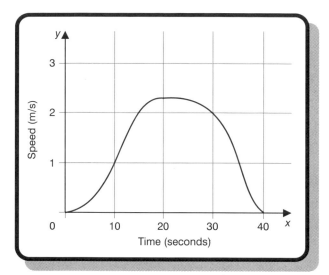

7 The graph of $y = \sin x$ is illustrated below.

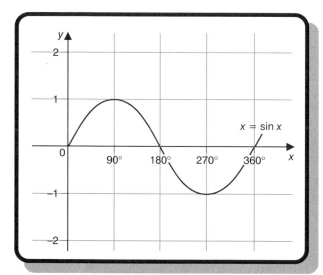

a) Giving your answer to the nearest degree, find two solutions for the equation $\sin x = 0.67$.

b) On the same axes, sketch the curve $y = 2\sin x$.

8 Find a value of x, to the nearest degree, in the range $180° < x < 360°$, such that $\cos x = 0.642$.

9 It is believed that y is related to x in such a way that $y = px^2 + q$, where p and q are constants.

x	1	2	3	4	5
y	8	17	32	53	80

On the axes below, draw the graph of y against x^2. Use your graph to estimate the values of p and q.

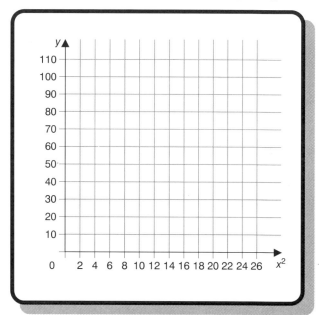

10 A concert hall in Ruritania can seat at most 900 people. Let x represent the number of men and y the number of women. No more than twice as many women as men may attend. Women are charged R\$14 and men R\$6. Enter this information on the graph provided, leaving the required region unshaded.

The concert needs to raise at least R\$8400. Find the number of tickets sold to men and women respectively which would maximise profit.

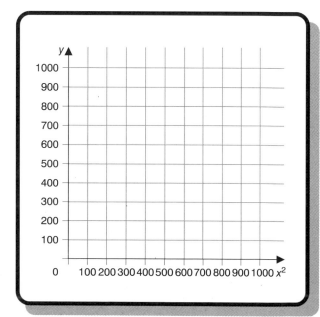

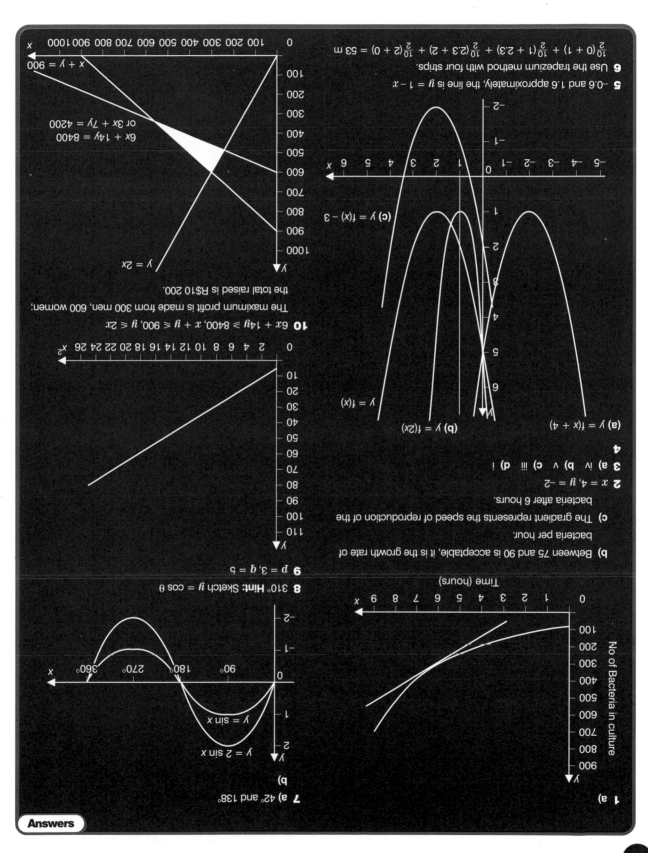

6 Use the trapezium method with four strips.
$\frac{10}{2}(0+1) + \frac{10}{2}(1+2.3) + \frac{10}{2}(2.3+2) + \frac{10}{2}(2+0) = 53$ m

5 −0.6 and 1.6 approximately, the line is $y = 1 - x$

(c) $y = f(x) - 3$

$y = f(x)$

(a) $y = f(x + 4)$ **(b)** $y = f(2x)$

4
3 a) iv   **b)** v   **c)** iii   **d)** i
2 $x = 4$, $y = -2$
c) The gradient represents the speed of reproduction of the bacteria after 6 hours.
b) Between 75 and 90 is acceptable, it is the growth rate of bacteria per hour.
1 a)

No of Bacteria in culture / Time (hours)

10 $6x + 14y \geqslant 8400$, $x + y \leqslant 900$, $y \leqslant 2x$
The maximum profit is made from 300 men, 600 women; the total raised is R$10 200.

$x + y = 900$

$6x + 14y = 8400$ or $3x + 7y = 4200$

$y = 2x$

9 $p = 3$, $q = 5$
8 310° Hint: Sketch $y = \cos \theta$
7 a) 42° and 138°
b)

$y = \sin x$

$y = 2 \sin x$

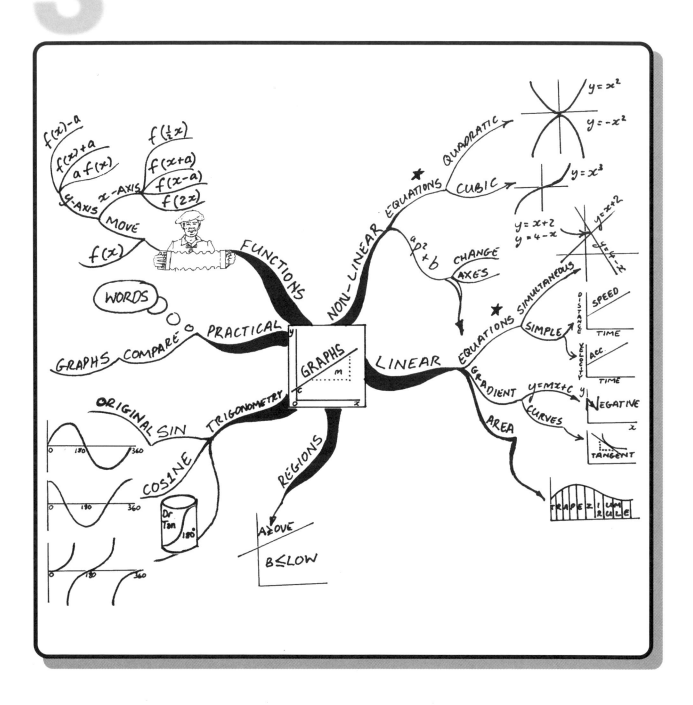

review

How much have you learnt?

Tick off each topic in the list when you are confident you can cope with it.

- Identify the gradient and *y*-intercept from the equation of a straight line.
- Draw a tangent to a curve at a given point.
- Find the area under a graph.
- Identify what the area under a graph represents.
- Solve simultaneous equations graphically.
- Sketch quadratic equations.
- Convert a non-linear graph to a linear graph by changing variables.
- Find values of the constants in a non-linear function.
- Transform functions.
- Draw trigonometric graphs.
- Find the values of an unknown, in a given range, that satisfy a trigonometric equation.
- Solve problems using linear programming.
- Find a range of values that satisfy an algebraic inequality.
- Maximise or minimise an expression.
- Recognise graphs of mathematical equations.

Algebra

4

Which of these feathers are in *your* cap?

- Formula rearrangement
- Equations with powers and roots
- Simultaneous equations (Algebraic solutions)
- Expanding double brackets
- Factorising quadratic expressions
- Solving quadratic equations
- Inequalities
- Iteration
- Sequences

preview

By the end of this chapter you will be able to:

- factorise simple algebraic expressions

- factorise quadratic equations when the coefficient of x^2 is 1

- factorise quadratic equations when the coefficient of x^2 is not 1

- rearrange formulae

- manipulate equations and formulae with powers and roots

- solve simultaneous equations algebraically

- multiply out brackets

- solve inequalities involving powers of x

- factorise the difference of two squares

- solve equations by iteration

- find the nth terms of sequences

- find the next terms in Fibonacci sequences

- recognise triangular numbers

Remember:

Variables are letters such as x or y which are used to represent numbers.

Expressions are statements involving variables, such as $x^2 + 1$.

An **equation** is a relationship between expressions with an equals sign in it, such as $x^2 + 1 = 2x$.

We're counting on you to be able to do these questions.

Exercise 4.1

1 Find x where:
- **a)** $5x + 3 = 23$
- **b)** $2x - 5 = 17$
- **c)** $4 = 16 - 3x$
- **d)** $3x + 10 = 4$
- **e)** $6x - 1 = 2$
- **f)** $x + 1 = 11$
- **g)** $4x + 7 = 2x + 37$
- **h)** $x - 1 = 4x - 10$
- **i)** $2(x - 1) + 5(x + 2) = 57$
- **j)** $3(1 - x) - 4(2x - 1) = 73$

2 Simplify these.
- **a)** $\dfrac{3x^2 \times 2x^4}{x^5}$
- **b)** $\dfrac{12y^3}{8x^2y}$
- **c)** $\dfrac{12y^2}{6y^3}$
- **d)** $5x^3 + 3x^3 + 2x^2$
- **e)** $a(a + b) - b(a - b)$
- **f)** $b \times (-b^2)$
- **g)** $x^2 - 2x(1 - 2x)$
- **h)** $(x^3)^4$

3 Write the following as single fractions.
- **a)** $\dfrac{1}{u} + \dfrac{1}{v}$
- **b)** $\dfrac{x}{2} + \dfrac{x + 2}{4}$

Make sure that you can do these questions. If you have trouble with any of them, ask for extra help from your teacher. Ask for some similar questions, to try.

The **coefficient** is the number that multiplies the variable. For example, in the expression $2x^2 - x + 4$, the coefficient of x^2 is 2 and the coefficient of x is –1. The 4 is called the **constant**.

Factorising using single brackets

Factorising means splitting a number into its factors. When you factorise you need to find the highest common factors, i.e. the biggest numbers or letters that 'go into' all the terms.

Example 4.1

Find the highest common factor of each pair of numbers.

a) 4 and 10

b) 20 and 5

c) a and a^2

d) y^2 and y^3

Solution

a) 2 $4 = 2 \times 2$, $10 = 5 \times 2$, so the highest common factor, or HCF of 4 and 10 is 2.

b) 5 $20 = 4 \times 5$, $5 = 1 \times 5$, so the HCF of 20 and 5 is 5.

c) $a^2 = a \times a$, so the HCF of a and a^2 is a.

d) $y^2 = y \times y$ and $y^3 = y \times y \times y$, so their HCF is $y \times y = y^2$.

Example 4.2

Factorise $10z^2b - 6za$.

Solution

Start with the 10 and the 6. Their HCF is 2.

Write the 2 outside the brackets.

$2(\qquad)$

If you were simplifying, as you did in the section above, you would have to have 5 and 3 in the brackets in order to multiply out correctly.

$2(5z^2b - 3za)$

Inside the brackets you still have z^2 and z. Their HCF is z, so you can write that outside the brackets as well. As you must be able to multiply out the factorised expression to find the original again, the solution is:

$10z^2b - 6za = 2z(5zb - 3a)$

The letters a and b each appear in one term only, so they stay inside the brackets.

Example 4.3

Factorise $6x^2y + 18xy^2$ fully.

Solution

The HCF of 6 and 18 is 6.

$6x^2y + 18xy^2 = 6(x^2y + 3xy^2)$

If it helps, you can cross out the factors as you go along.

$6x^2y + 18xy^2 = 6(x^2y + 3xy^2)$

or

$6x^2y + 18x^2 = 6(x^2y + 3xy^2)$

The HCF of x^2 and x is x.

$6(x^2y + 3xy^2) = 6x(xy + 3y^2)$

or

$6(x^2y + 3xy^2) = 6x(xy + 3y^2)$

The HCF of y and y^2 is y.

$6x(xy + 3y^2) = 6xy(x + 3y)$

or

$6x(xy + 3y^2) = 6xy(x + 3y)$

So
$$6x^2y + 18xy^2 = 6xy(x + 3y)$$

Check your answer by multiplying out the brackets.

Example 4.4

Factorise $12a^2b^2 - 4ab$ fully.

Solution

The HCF of 12 and 4 is 4.

$12a^2b^2 - 4ab = 4(3a^2b^2 - ab)$
or
$12a^2b^2 - 4ab = 4(3a^2b^2 - ab)$

The HCF of a^2 and a is a.

$4(3a^2b^2 - ab) = 4a(3ab^2 - b)$
or
$4(3a^2b^2 - ab) = 4a(3ab^2 - b)$

The HCF of b^2 and b is b.

So $4a(3ab^2 - b) = 4ab(3ab - 1)$
or
$4a(3ab^2 - b) = 4ab(3ab - 1)$

If all the factors of a term are taken outside the bracket, you have to replace them inside the bracket with a 1, so that when you multiply out the bracket you will get back to your original expression.

Exercise 4.2

Factorise the following expressions.

1 $16ab + 10bc$

2 $4c^2 - 2ac$

3 $10a^2b^2 - 5a$

Formula rearrangement

Our characters are using short cuts to make life easier.

Meet Chuckwagon Charlie, Underhand Luke and Buffalo Lil
When Chuckwagon Charlie chucks a +2 on to the other side and changes sign, he is really subtracting 2 from both sides of the equation.

It's Underhand Luke who multiplies or divides every term on both sides when changing '× 3' to '÷ 3'.

Buffalo Lil lassos the term containing the required subject. If this term is negative, she takes it over to the other side to make the coefficient positive.

Linear equations where the subject appears once

Example 4.5

Make x the subject of the formula $y = mx + c$.

Solution

Buffalo Lil lassos the term in x. This is positive, so she leaves it where it is.

$y = mx + c$

Chuckwagon Charlie chucks the c over to the other side, making it $-c$.

$y - c = mx$

Underhand Luke divides everything on both sides of the equation by m.

$$\frac{y - c}{m} = x$$

$$x = \frac{y - c}{m}$$

Example 4.6

Make y the subject of the formula $ab - ky = c$.

Solution

Buffalo Lil lassos the term in y, and as it's negative, she moves it to the other side of the equation. It becomes positive on the other side.

$ab = c + ky$

Now the guys come in to help with the lasso side. Chuckwagon Charlie chucks the '$+c$' across to the other side. At the same time, for the terms he moves, he changes the operation on them. Plus becomes minus and vice versa.

$ab - c = ky$

At the moment, y is multiplied by k. Underhand Luke – as with Chuckwagon Charlie – reverses the operation and divides everything on both sides by k.

$$\frac{ab - c}{k} = y \quad \text{or} \quad y = \frac{ab - c}{k}$$

Linear equations where the required subject appears twice

Example 4.7

Rearrange $2hx = kx + m$ to make x the subject of the formula.

Solution

Buffalo Lil lassos the two terms with x, and takes them both on one side.

$2hx - kx = m$

She now takes the x out of the lasso by factorising.

$x(2h - k) = m$

Underhand Luke divides everything on both sides by the terms in the lasso.

$$x = \frac{m}{2h - k}$$

Example 4.8

Make r the subject of the formula $rh - A = \pi rl$.

Solution

Buffalo Lil lassos the terms containing r.

$rh - A = \pi rl$

Then she takes them over to one side.

$rh - A - \pi rl = 0$ or $-A = \pi rl - rh$

If there are any terms not containing r on the lasso side, then Chuckwagon Charlie will come along and chuck 'em over.

$rh - \pi rl = A$ or $-A = \pi rl - rh$

Buffalo Lil factorises the r outside the lasso.

$r(h - \pi l) = A$ $\qquad$ $-A = r(\pi l - h)$

Then Underhand Luke divides everything on both sides by the coefficient of r.

$r = \dfrac{A}{h - \pi l}$ $\qquad$ or $\qquad$ $r = \dfrac{-A}{\pi l - h}$

Equations where the required subject appears in the denominator

Example 4.9

Make x the subject of the formula $b + \dfrac{1}{x} = a$.

Solution

Underhand Luke grabs the x and multiplies everything by x.

$bx + 1 = ax$

Buffalo Lil lassos the two terms containing x, and moves them to the same side of the equation (the term without x goes to the other side).

either $bx - ax = -1$ or $1 = ax - bx$

Buffalo Lil factorises x outside the equation, leaving either $(b - a)$ or $(a - b)$ in the lasso.

$x(b - a) = -1$ $\qquad$ or $\qquad$ $1 = x(a - b)$

Underhand Luke takes the term in the lasso over to the other side, dividing by it.

$x = -\dfrac{1}{b - a}$ $\qquad$ or $\qquad$ $x = \dfrac{1}{a - b}$

Equations with powers and roots

Example 4.10

Rearrange $v^2 = u^2 - 2as$ to make u the subject of the formula.

Solution

Buffalo Lil lassos the term containing u,

$v^2 = u^2 - 2as$

whilst Chuckwagon Charlie chucks the other term across.

$v^2 + 2as = u^2$

Now Buffalo Lil tightens the noose around the u^2, and realises she must get rid of the squared sign.

Underhand Luke reverses it by taking the square root of everything on both sides.

$\sqrt{v^2 + 2as} = u$

Example 4.11

Rewrite the formula $T = 2\pi\sqrt{\dfrac{l}{g}}$ to give l in terms of T and g.

Solution

Buffalo Lil lassos the term with l in it, and gradually tightens the noose.

2π is the first item outside the lasso, and Underhand Luke lugs it across to the other side to divide by 2π.

$\dfrac{T}{2\pi} = \sqrt{\dfrac{l}{g}}$

The noose is further tightened to take the $\sqrt{\ }$ sign outside the formula.

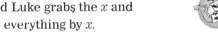

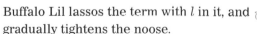

Underhand Luke lugs it across and squares the whole of the other side.

$$\left(\frac{T}{2\pi}\right)^2 = \frac{l}{g}$$

Finally, the noose is tightened to reveal the g. This is lugged across to give the final answer.

$$g\left(\frac{T}{2\pi}\right)^2 = l \quad \text{or} \quad \frac{gT^2}{4\pi^2} = l$$

Be careful when squaring or finding the square root:

$(2\pi)^2 = 4\pi^2$, not $2\pi^2$

$(x + y)^2$ is not the same as $x^2 + y^2$

$\sqrt{x^2 + y^2}$ is not the same as $x + y$.

Exercise 4.3

Rewrite the following equations in terms of the variable in brackets.

1 $d = b - ac$ $\qquad\qquad (c)$

2 $uv = 2v + w$ $\qquad\qquad (v)$

3 $a = \dfrac{b}{c} + d$ $\qquad\qquad (c)$

4 $V = 2 - \pi rhl$ $\qquad\qquad (h)$

5 $s = ut + \frac{1}{2}at^2$ $\qquad\qquad (a)$

6 $y = \dfrac{3x}{x - 2}$ $\qquad\qquad (x)$

7 $A = \pi r\sqrt{u + v}$ $\qquad\qquad (u)$

8 $\dfrac{1}{x} + b = a$ $\qquad\qquad (x)$

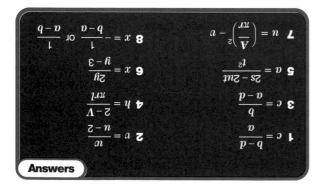

Answers

$$\mathbf{1}\ c = \frac{b-d}{a} \qquad \mathbf{2}\ v = \frac{w}{u-2}$$

$$\mathbf{3}\ c = \frac{b}{a-d} \qquad \mathbf{4}\ h = \frac{2-V}{\pi r l}$$

$$\mathbf{5}\ a = \frac{2s-2ut}{t^2} \qquad \mathbf{6}\ x = \frac{2y}{y-3}$$

$$\mathbf{7}\ u = \left(\frac{A}{\pi r}\right)^2 - v \qquad \mathbf{8}\ x = \frac{1}{a-b}\ \text{or}\ \frac{1}{a-b}$$

TAKE A BREAK

You've worked hard and you deserve one.

Simultaneous equations

These are two equations involving two variables (usually x and y), for which you are asked to find the values of x and y which satisfy both equations.

With simultaneous equations you need to find x and y, so:

Simultaneous Equations are SEXY.

In the GCSE there are two different ways of solving them – algebraically and graphically. The graphical method is shown in Chapter 3, Graphs.

Remember: The **coefficient** is the number multiplying a variable. For example, in the expression $x^2 - 2x - 1$ the coefficient of x^2 is 1, the coefficient of x is –2 and the constant is –1.

Algebraic solution

We shall look at two ways of solving simultaneous equations using algebra – elimination and substitution.

Method 1 – elimination

This is the most common method, and is used when all the variables are on the same side of the equations.

Example 4.12

Solve the following simultaneous equations.

$$4x + 2y = 22$$

$$3x + 2y = 19$$

Solution

1 One of the variables must have the same coefficient in both equations (ignoring whether they are positive or negative). In our example there is a $2y$ in both equations.

2 If the signs are the same, you take away one equation from the other.
If the signs are opposite you add (plus) them.

*Remember: STOP **S**ame **T**ake, **O**pposite **P**lus*

3 In our example, both $2y$ terms are positive (same sign), so we must take away.

Box the terms that will cancel out.

$$4x + 2y = 22$$
$$\underline{3x + 2y = 19}$$
$$x \qquad = 3 \qquad (4x - 3x = x, 22 - 19 = 3)$$

Remember: Simultaneous Equations are SEXY – you need to find both x and y.

Now use the easier equation to find y.

$$3x + 2y = 19$$
$$9 + 2y = 19 \qquad (because\ 3x = 3 \times 3 = 9)$$
$$2y = 10$$
$$y = 5$$

Check using the other equation ($4x + 2y = 22$).

$$4 \times 3 + 2 \times 5 = 22$$

Example 4.13

Solve these equations.

$$3x + 2y = 16 \qquad \mathbf{1}$$
$$x + y = 5 \qquad \mathbf{2}$$

Solution

1 Ignoring the signs, are the coefficients of either variable the same? No!

So we must multiply the equation with the lower coefficient to make the coefficients of either x or y the same (ignoring signs). As we have chosen to eliminate y, we have multiplied the second equation by 2 (if eliminating x, you would have to multiply it by 3).

$$3x + 2y = 16 \qquad \mathbf{1}$$
$$\underline{2x + 2y = 10} \qquad \mathbf{2 \times 2}$$
$$x \qquad = 6$$

Using STOP, we've subtracted as the signs of the ys are the same.

Remembering SEXY, we need to find y, so substitute x back into the easier of the two original equations.

$$x + y = 5$$
$$6 + y = 5$$
$$y = -1$$

Check in equation **1** $\quad 3 \times 6 + 2 \times -1 = 16$

This is true so your answers for x and y are true.

Sometimes you have to multiply both equations to get the same coefficient in x or y. If the equations were:

$$2x + 3y = 5 \qquad \mathbf{1}$$
$$3x - 5y = 2 \qquad \mathbf{2}$$

we could multiply **1** by 3 and **2** by 2 to get $6x$ in both.

Example 4.14

Solve these equations.

$$5x - 4y = 32$$
$$3x + 4y = 0$$

Solution

Ignoring the signs, the coefficients of y are the same.

STOP   Same Take, Opposite Plus

The signs are opposite for the $4y$s so the equations must be added.

$$5x - 4y = 32$$
$$\underline{3x + 4y = 0}$$
$$8x = 32$$
$$x = 4$$

Remember SEXY – you must find y.

Use the simpler second equation, $3x + 4y = 0$.

$12 + 4y = 0$

$4y = -12$

$y = -3$

Check in the first equation, $5x - 4y = 32$.

$5 \times 4 - 4 \times -3 = 32$

using your calculator if necessary.

Exercise 4.4

Solve the following simultaneous equations.

1 $3x + 2y = 31$

$x + 2y = 21$

2 $12x - 5y = 79$

$9x + 5y = 68$

3 $5x + 4y = 38$

$3x + 5y = 41$

4 $6x + 5y = 31$

$3x + 4y = 23$

Answers

4 $x = 1, y = 5$

3 $x = 2, y = 7$

2 $x = 7, y = 1$

1 $x = 5, y = 8$

Method 2 – substitution

Use this method when x and y are on different sides in at least one equation.

Example 4.15

Solve these equations.

$5x - 3y = 5$ **1**

$x = y - 3$ **2**

Solution

We can solve this by simply replacing the x in the first equation by $y - 3$ from the second equation, remembering to bracket it.

$5(y - 3) - 3y = 5$

$5y - 15 - 3y = 5$

$2y - 15 = 5$

$2y = 20$

$y = 10$

Using **2**:

$x = 10 - 3$

$x = 7$

Check in **1**: $5 \times 7 - 3 \times 10 = 5$

Exercise 4.5

Solve these equations.

1 $5x + 3y = 27$

$y = x - 7$

2 $5x - y = 15$

$y = 2x - 9$

3 $4x - 3y = -1$

$y = 2x - 1$

Answers

3 $x = 2, y = 3$

2 $x = 2, y = -5$

1 $x = 6, y = -1$

TAKE A BREAK

Time for another break. This chapter is quite challenging. Don't try to rush it.

Multiplying out (expanding) double brackets

*We use **FOIL** – **F**irst **O**uter **I**nner **L**ast to expand double brackets. Use your own method if you prefer.*

Example 4.16

Expand these brackets.

$(x + 1)(2x + 3)$

Solution

Using FOIL	First	Outer	Inner	Last
	↓	↓	↓	↓
$(x + 1)(2x + 3)$	$= 2x^2$	$+ 3x$	$+ 2x$	$+ 3$
	$= 2x^2 + 5x + 3$			

A common mistake is to add instead of multiply the last terms.

Exercise 4.6

Expand the following.

1 $(x + 3)(x - 2)$

2 $(x - 1)(x + 1)$

3 $(4 - x)(x + 7)$

4 $(2x - 1)(3x - 5)$

5 $(2x - 5)^2$

Linear inequalities

○ means not including

● means including

$-2 \leq x < 5$ means x is between -2 and 5, includes -2 but not 5.

On a number line:

Inequalities are very similar to equations, but with two important differences.

1 If you swap the entire left and right-hand sides then the inequality reverses.

2 If you multiply or divide by a negative number, then the inequality sign is reversed.

Example 4.17

Find the range of values of x for which $3 - 2x < 7$.

Solution

Method 1 – taking the $2x$ over to make the coefficient positive

$3 < 2x + 7$

$2x + 7 > 3$ Swapping the sides and reversing the inequality (Rule 1).

$2x > -4$

$x > -2$

Method 2 – dividing by -2

$3 - 2x < 7$

$-2x < 4$

$x > -2$ The inequality reverses when dividing by a negative number (Rule 2).

Example 4.18

Find the largest integer for which $7x + 1 < 46$.

Solution

Solving the inequality gives $x < 6.43$.

The largest integer that satisfies this inequality is 6.

Example 4.19

Find the range of values of x for which
$2x + 1 < 3x + 7 \leqslant 2x + 16$.

Solution

Solving $2x + 5 < 3x + 7$ gives $x > -2$.

Solving $3x + 7 \leqslant 2x + 16$ gives $x \leqslant 9$.

To satisfy both inequalities, x must be B⩽TW⩽⩽N -2 and 9.

The range is $-2 < x \leqslant 9$.

Exercise 4.7

Find the range of values of x which satisfy the following inequalities.

1 $5 - 4x \leqslant 11$

2 $2 - 7x > 10 - 9x$

3 $x + 4 < 9 + 3x$

4 $x - 2 \leqslant 4x + 1 < 2x + 7$

4 $-1 \leqslant x > 3$
3 $x > -2.5$
2 $x > 4$
1 $x \geqslant -1.5$

Answers

Inequalities involving x²

Remember B⩽TW⩽⩽N for $x^2 \leqslant$ or $x^2 <$ questions, and ⩽⩾UTSI|⩾E for $x^2 \geqslant$ and $x^2 >$ questions.

Example 4.20

Find the range of values of x for which:

a) $x^2 \leqslant 4$ **b)** $x^2 > 4$.

Solution

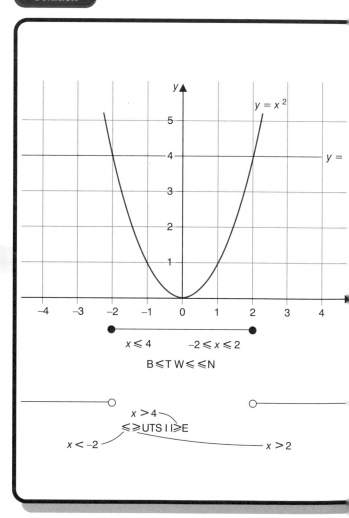

a) From the graph, the $y = x^2$ curve is below (i.e. less than) the $y = 4$ line when x is B⩽TW⩽⩽N -2 and 2.

$-2 \leqslant x \leqslant 2$

b) From the graph, $y = x^2$ is above $y = 4$ ⩽⩾UTSI⩾E –2 and 2. Therefore $x < -2$ and $x > 2$.

These must be written as two separate inequalities as the regions are different.

Exercise 4.8

Find the range of values of x which satisfy these inequalities.

1 $x^2 \geqslant 25$

2 $x^2 < 9$

3 $2x^2 \geqslant 32$

4 $x^2 + 3 \leqslant 39$

Answers

4 $-6 \leqslant x \leqslant 6$

3 $x \leqslant -4, x \geqslant 4$

2 $-3 < x < 3$

1 $x \leqslant -5, x \geqslant 5$

Quadratic expressions

Factorising into two brackets

Factorising when the coefficient of x^2 is 1

Example 4.21

Factorise these expressions.

a) $x^2 + 6x + 5$ **b)** $x^2 + 3x - 10$ **c)** $x^2 - 5x + 6$

Solution

a) $x^2 + 6x + 5$

We need two numbers that multiply together to give 5 and add together to give 6.

i.e. 1 and 5

$x^2 + 6x + 5 = (x + 5)(x + 1)$

b) $x^2 + 3x - 10$

We need two numbers with product –10 and sum 3.

The signs must be different, with the larger number positive, because the term in x ($3x$) is positive.

$x^2 + 3x - 10 = (x + 5)(x - 2)$

If you have difficulty, write down all numbers with product 10.

c) $x^2 - 5x + 6$

We need two numbers with product 6 and sum –5, since the expression has a positive product, but a negative x-coefficient.

Therefore the two numbers must be negative.

$x^2 - 5x + 6 = (x - 3)(x - 2)$

Exercise 4.9

Factorise the following expressions.

1 $x^2 - x - 12$

2 $x^2 - 9x + 8$

3 $x^2 + 2x - 15$

Answers

3 $(x + 5)(x - 3)$

2 $(x - 8)(x - 1)$

1 $(x - 4)(x + 3)$

Just to recap

1 Start by looking at the sign of the constant.

2 If it is positive, both brackets have the same sign. If it is negative the brackets will have different signs.

Turn to page 70 for a summary on factorising quadratics of this form.

Factorising when the coefficient of x^2 is greater then 1

Example 4.22

Factorise $3x^2 + 13x - 10$.

Solution

The coefficient of x^2 can only be the product of $3x$ and x. So write these at the start of the brackets.

$(3x \quad)(x \quad)$

Now write all the pairs of numbers with product 10: 1×10; 2×5.

Experiment to see which makes the coefficient of x equal to 13.

$3x^2 + 13x - 10 = (3x - 2)(x + 5)$

Exercise 4.10

Factorise the following expressions.

1 $5x^2 - 7x - 6$

2 $3x^2 + x - 10$

3 $2x^2 - 11x + 12$

4 $3x^2 + 11x + 6$

5 $2x^2 + x - 10$

6 $4x^2 + 4x + 1$

Answers

1 $(5x + 3)(x - 2)$
2 $(3x - 5)(x + 2)$
3 $(2x - 3)(x - 4)$
4 $(3x + 2)(x + 3)$
5 $(2x + 5)(x - 2)$
6 $(2x + 1)^2$

Difference of two squares

These are quadratic expressions, but they have no term in x, and the two terms are separated by a minus sign.

Example 4.23

Factorise these expressions.

a) $x^2 - y^2$ **b)** $100a^2 - 49b^2$

c) $a^2 - 1$ **d)** $18x^2 - 8y^2$

Solution

a) $x^2 - y^2 = (x - y)(x + y)$, or of course $(x + y)(x - y)$

b) $100a^2 - 49b^2 = (10a - 7b)(10a + 7b)$

c) $a^2 - 1 = (a - 1)(a + 1)$

d) $18x^2 - 8y^2 = 2(9x^2 - 4y^2)$

$$= 2(3x - 2y)(3x + 2y)$$

Exercise 4.11

Factorise the following expressions.

1 $b^2 - a^2$

2 $1 - 9x^2$

3 $4a^2 - 25$

4 $3x^2 - 12a^2$

Answers

1 $(b - a)(b + a)$
2 $(1 - 3x)(1 + 3x)$
3 $(2a - 5)(2a + 5)$
4 $3(x^2 - 4a^2) = 3(x - 2a)(x + 2a)$

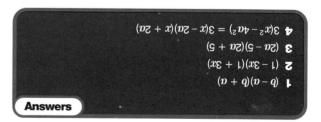

TAKE A BREAK

Quadratic equations

Quadratic equations are of the form
$ax^2 + bx + c = 0$.

For example, $2x^2 + x - 4 = 0$ is a quadratic equation.

Solution of quadratic equations

The three most common ways of solving quadratic equations for GCSE are:

1 factorising

2 quadratic formula

3 graphically (see Chapter 3, Graphs for this method).

Solution of quadratics – method 1

After taking all terms on to one side and factorising, equate each bracket to zero and solve.

For example $x^2 + 6x + 5 = 0$

$$(x + 5)(x + 1) = 0$$

When the product of two numbers is zero, one or the other must be zero.

So either $x + 5 = 0$ or $x + 1 = 0$

$x = -5$ $x = -1$

You must have a zero on the right-hand side of the equation to use this method.

Also, if you have a negative coefficient of x^2, take all terms on to the other side of the equation to make the coefficient positive.

Solution of quadratics – method 2

You may have to use the formula for solving quadratics.

$$x = \frac{-b \pm \sqrt{b^2 - 4ac}}{2a}$$

Don't worry, you do not need to learn this – it'll be on the *Information and formulae sheet* of your exam paper.

Use this method if:

- the question asks you to give your answer to a certain number of decimal places

- the equation looks difficult to factorise.

Exercise 4.12

1 Find the values of x which satisfy these equations.
   a) $x^2 + 8x = -15$ **b)** $2x^2 - 11x + 5 = 0$
   c) $x^2 + 24x = 25$ **d)** $x^2 - 9 = 0$
   e) $x^2 = 25$

2 Find the values of x in the following questions, correct to two decimal places.
   a) $3x^2 - 11x + 4 = 0$ **b)** $4x^2 - 17x + 1 = 0$
   c) $2x^2 + 8x = 3$ **d)** $3x^2 + 1 = 9x$
   e) $6 - x^2 - 10x = 0$

Answers

e) $x = -10.57, x = 0.57$
d) $x = 0.12, x = 2.88$
c) $x = 0.35, x = -4.35$
b) $x = 4.19, x = 0.06$
2 a) $x = 3.26, x = 0.41$

e) $x = -5, x = 5$
d) $x = -3, x = 3$
c) $x = -25, x = 1$
b) $x = 0.5, x = 5$
1 a) $x = -5, x = -3$

TAKE A BREAK

Definitely time for another break!
There's a bit more hard work coming up.

4

Iteration

Iteration is a way of finding the next term in a sequence.

The nth term of a sequence u is usually referred to as u_n (although different letters may be used to denote the sequence e.g. p_n, v_n, etc.)

The first term of a sequence u is u_1.

The second term of a sequence is u_2.

u_n is the nth term.

u_{n+1} is the $(n + 1)$th term i.e. the term after the nth.

u_{n-1} is the $(n - 1)$th term i.e. the term before the nth.

The solution of an iterative formula may also be described as a limit.

Example 4.24

A sequence is given by:

$$u_{n+1} = \frac{8}{u_n + 2}$$

$$u_1 = 3$$

a) Find u_2, u_3 and u_4.

b) What do you think will happen to u_n as n gets larger?

c) Solve $x = \dfrac{8}{x + 2}$ to show that your answer to **(b)** is correct.

Solution

a) $u_2 = \dfrac{8}{3 + 2} = 1.6$

$u_3 = \dfrac{8}{1.6 + 2} = 2.2$

$u_4 = \dfrac{8}{2.2 + 2} = 1.9$

b) You could try $n = 5, 6$, etc. to show that u_n tends towards 2 as n gets larger.

c) You can see that the formula is almost identical to the iteration formula. You will find that this is a quadratic equation. The positive solution leads to the answer to both **(c)** and **(b)**.

$x(x + 2) = 8$

$x^2 + 2x = 8$

$x^2 + 2x - 8 = 0$ To solve you must have a 0 on the right-hand side.

$(x + 4)(x - 2) = 0$

$x = -4$ or $x = 2$

Exercise 4.13

1 a) Show that the equation $x^2 - 6x + 2 = 0$ may be rewritten as $x = 6 - \dfrac{2}{x}$.

b) Using the iterative formula $x_{n+1} = 6 - \dfrac{2}{x_n}$ and starting with $x_1 = 6$, find a solution of the quadratic equation, correct to two decimal places.

2 a) Show that $2x^2 + x - 7 = 0$ may be rewritten as $x = \sqrt{\dfrac{7 - x}{2}}$.

b) Use the iterative formula $u_{n+1} = \sqrt{\dfrac{7 - u_n}{2}}$ with an initial value of $u_1 = 3$ to find an apparent limit, correct to two decimal places.

Answers

b) 1.64

2 a) $x^2 = \dfrac{7 - x}{2}$ and take square root on both sides.

b) 5.65

1 a) $x^2 = 6x - 2$, then divide both sides by x

If you cannot show that, for example, $2x^2 + x - 7 = 0$ can be rewritten as $x = \sqrt{\dfrac{7 - x}{2}}$,

start by writing $x = \sqrt{\dfrac{7 - x}{2}}$

at the bottom, above it write $x^2 = \dfrac{7 - x}{2}$,

then multiply both sides by 2, and so on, until you get to the original equation.

Sequences

Meet DINO and COSTAS

Let's introduce our Greek bartenders, DINO and COSTAS.

DINO likes things laid out with equal spacing,

whereas COSTAS likes the differences to get larger.

Sequences with equal spacing

Example 4.25

Study the sequence 9, 16, 23, 30, ...

a) What is the difference between consecutive terms?

b) What is the next term in the sequence?

c) What is the nth term?

d) What is the 25th term?

Solution

a) The difference between consecutive terms
$= 30 - 23 = 23 - 16 = 16 - 9 = 7$

b) The next term is $30 + 7 = 37$.

c) Here we can use DINO, as the numbers are evenly spaced, with a difference of 7. Put a ring before the first term.

$\bigcirc$ 9, 16, 23, 30, ...

What number would go in here if there were a number before the 9?

$9 - 7 = 2$

$\textcircled{2}$ 9, 16, 23, 30, ...

DI stands for the difference (7), N stands for n and O stands for the number in the ring (2).

DINO gives $7n + 2$.

Check: If you put $n = 1$, you should get the first term, $7 \times 1 + 2 = 9$; $n = 2$ gives the second term, 16, etc.

The nth term is $7n + 2$.

d) What is the 25th term?

Put $n = 25$, which gives $7 \times 25 + 2 = 177$

Questions often ask for the nth term after they ask for the 25th term, but it is easier to use DINO first then substitute $n = 25$ to find the 25th term.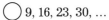

If you are asked to find n for a given term, find the formula using DINO and then equate it to the given value.

Unequally spaced sequences

Example 4.26

The following numbers form a sequence.

3, 6, 11, 18, ...

a) What is the next term in the sequence?

b) What is the nth term in the sequence?

Solution

a) Look at the differences between the terms.

3, 5, 7, ...

It can be seen that the difference increases by 2 every term, so the next difference must be 9. The next term must be $18 + 9 = 27$.

3, 6, 11, 18, 27

b) COSTAS may be used as the differences are not equal.

COSTAS stands for

Cube Or Square Times, Add, Subtract

Write the sequence down, with the number of each term above it.

n	1	2	3	4
u_n	3	6	11	18

First try squaring the n (as squaring is easier than cubing), and comparing to see if you can see a link between the squared numbers and each term. (If you can't, then you can try cubing them.)

n	1	2	3	4
n^2	1	4	9	16
u_n	3	6	11	18

You can see that you have to add 2 to n^2 to get the term. So the nth term is $n^2 + 2$.

If your sequence is given as a series of fractions, look for DINO or COSTAS in the numerators and in the demoninators. Treat them as two different sequences.

Example 4.27

Find an expression for the nth term in the following sequence.

2, 16, 54, 128, ...

Solution

Write the numbers 1, 2, 3, 4 above the corresponding terms, leaving a space in between.

n	1	2	3	4
	2	16	54	128

Using COSTAS, start by squaring n.

n	1	2	3	4
n^2	1	4	9	16
	2	16	54	128

Comparing the n^2 line with the bottom line and using the TAS of COSTAS (which stands for Times, Add, Subtract), there is no way of finding a link between the numbers in the two lines. You don't need the n^2 line, so put a line through it.

We've used the first S from COSTAS, so now we try the C (cube).

n	1	2	3	4
n^2	~~1~~	~~4~~	~~9~~	~~16~~
n^3	1	8	27	64
	2	16	54	128

Using the TAS of COSTAS (which stands for Times, Add, Subtract), you can clearly see that to find the bottom line, you would multiply the numbers in the n^3 row by 2.

So the nth term is $2 \times n^3$, or $2n^3$.

The 3–5–7 sequence (a quicker method for some of COSTAS' sequences)

This works for sequences which have differences between terms of 3 then 5 then 7 etc.

n^2 is the sequence 1, 4, 9, 16, ... and the differences are 3, 5, 7, 9, ... so all the following sequences are based upon adding a number to this.

Example 4.28

Find the nth term of the sequence 10, 13, 18, 25, ...

Solution

The differences in the sequence are 3, 5, 7, ...

Subtracting 1 from the first term gives 9, so the nth term of the sequence is:

$n^2 + 9$

Example 4.29

Find an expression for the nth term of the sequence 5, 8, 13, 20, ...

Solution

The nth term is $n^2 + 4$. **Check** it for yourself.

Fibonacci sequences

These are sequences in which each term is the sum of the two previous terms.

Example 4.30

Find the next three terms in the sequence 1, 1, 2, 3, 5, 8, ...

Solution

Using the rule, the next three terms are
$8 + 5 = 13, 13 + 8 = 21, 21 + 13 = 34$.

Triangular numbers

1, 3, 6, 10, ... is the sequence of triangular numbers. The formula for the nth term is $\frac{1}{2}n(n + 1)$.

Exponential sequences

These are quite complicated. Each term is found by multiplying the previous term by a 'multiplier'.

For example, in the sequence 6, 12, 24, ... the multiplier is 2 and the first term is 6. The general formula is first term × (multiplier)$^{n-1}$ or $a \times m^{n-1}$.

Or try OMEN where O represents the previous term, m the multiplier and n the exponent or power.

OMEN's formula is $\frac{a}{m} \times m^n$.

The nth term in the example above will be

$6 \times 2^{n-1}$ or 3×2^n (be careful if $\frac{a}{m}$ gives a fractional answer).

Exercise 4.14

1 In the sequence 1, 4, 7, 10, 13, ...
   a) find the 16th term
   b) find which term gives the number 139
   c) give a formula for the nth term.

2 For the sequence 8, 11, 16, 23, 32, ... , find:
   a) the 14th term   **b)** the nth term.

3 For the sequence 5, 12, 19, 26, ... find:
   a) the 25th term   **b)** the nth term.

4 Find the nth term of the sequence 3, 12, 27, 48, ...

5 Find the next two terms in the sequence 2, 4, 6, 10, 16, ...

6 Find the nth term in the sequence 4, 11, 30, 67, ...

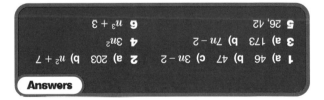

Answers

1 a) 46 **b)** 47 **c)** $3n - 2$ **2 a)** 203 **b)** $n^2 + 7$
3 a) 173 **b)** $7n - 2$
4 $3n^2$
5 26, 42   **6** $n^3 + 3$

TAKE A BREAK

Catch up on the mind maps. You could draw one up to help you hold on to all the hard work you've done on equations in this chapter.

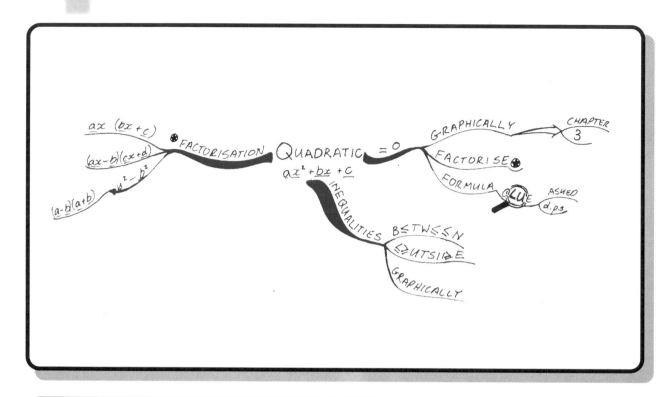

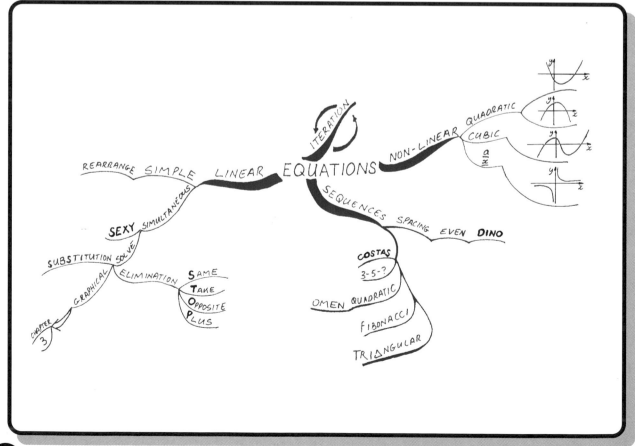

So you think you've got it sussed?

Exam-type questions 4

1 Here are the first five terms of a number sequence.
2, 8, 14, 20, 26
  a) Give a rule for the next term.
  b) Find the value of the 22nd term.
  c) Find an expression for the nth term.

2 Expand the following expressions.
  a) $(x - 1)(x + 6)$ **b)** $(6x + 1) - (x - 1)$
  c) $(c - d)(c + d)$ **d)** $(2x - 3)^2$

3 a) Rearrange the formula $V = \frac{4}{3}\pi r^3$ to give r in terms of V and π.
  b) Find the value of r when $V = 2017$.

4 Five pens and three rubbers cost 192 pence. Seven pens and six rubbers cost 303 pence.
  a) Write this information as two equations using x to represent the cost in pence of a pen, and y to represent the cost in pence of a rubber.
  b) Solve the equations to find x and y.

5 Factorise the following expressions.
  a) $8a^2b - 12ab^2$ **b)** $10b^2c^2 + 5bc$
  c) $x^2 - x + 6$ **d)** $2x^2 - 13x + 15$

6 a) Show that $x^{-1} = 3(x + 2)$ can be written as $3x^2 + 6x - 1 = 0$.
  b) Find the roots of this equation correct to 2 d.p.

7 Solve the following inequalities for x.
  a) $x^2 < 1$ **b)** $3x^2 > 12$ **c)** $x + 6 < 4x - 15$

8 The next term in the sequence
1, 1, 6, 21, …
can be found by adding the previous two terms and multiplying the result by 3. Give the next two numbers in the sequence.

9 a) Use the iteration formula $x_{n+1} = 4 - \dfrac{1}{x_n}$ to find a value for x correct to 2 d.p. Start by using $x_1 = 4$.
  b) Show how the formula can be rearranged to give $x^2 - 4x + 1 = 0$.
  c) Use a formula method to find the roots of this equation.

10 a) Factorise the expression $x^2 + x - 12$.
  b) Hence or otherwise solve the equation $x^2 + x = 12$.

11 Find the values of x and y in the following pairs of equations.
  a) $5x + 4y = 10$ **b)** $2x - 3y = 10$
     $y = x + 7$ $3x - 5y = 21$

12 a) Factorise the expression $a^2 - b^2$.
  b) Using the information from (**a**), and without a calculator, evaluate $52^2 - 49^2$. Show your working.

13 Find the nth term of each of these sequences.
  a) 7, 10, 15, 22, …   **b)** $\frac{5}{7}, \frac{8}{10}, \frac{11}{15}, \frac{14}{22}, …$

14 Use trial and improvement to find a value for x correct to 1 d.p. which satisfies the equation $x^2 - 2x = 95$. Start with the value $x = 8$.

15 Rearrange the following formulae to give x in terms of y and z.
  a) $y = \dfrac{z}{x + 1}$ **b)** $y = \dfrac{\pi\sqrt{x}}{z}$ **c)** $x^3 + 4 = yz$

Answers

15 a) $x = \dfrac{z - y}{y}$ or $x = \dfrac{z}{y} - 1$ **b)** $x = \left(\dfrac{\pi}{zy}\right)^2$ **c)** $x = \sqrt[3]{yz - 4}$

14 Rearrange to give $x = \dfrac{95}{x} + 2$, $x = 10.8$

13 a) $n^2 + 6$ **b)** $\dfrac{3n}{n^2 + 2}$

12 a) $(a - b)(a + b)$ **b)** $(52 - 49)(52 + 49) = 303$

11 a) $x = -2$, $y = 5$ **b)** $x = -13$, $y = -12$

Hint: Rearranging $x^2 + x$ gives 12 gives $x^2 + x - 12 = 0$

10 a) $(x + 4)(x - 3)$ **b)** $x = -4$, $x = 3$

  c) 3.73 and 0.27

by x to give $x^2 = 4x - 1$

$n + 1$ or n, and then multiply every term through

start by rewriting the iterative formula without

b) Hint: If you have trouble rearranging this equation,

9 a) 3.73

8 81 and 306

7 a) $-1 < x < 1$ **b)** $x < -2$, $x > 2$ **c)** $x > 7$

6 Remember $x^{-1} = \dfrac{1}{x}$ **b)** 0.15 and -2.15

  c) $(x - 3)(x + 2)$ **d)** $(2x - 3)(x - 5)$

5 a) $4ab(2a - 3b)$ **b)** $5bc(2bc + 1)$

  b) $x = 27$p, $y = 19$p

4 a) $5x + 3y = 192$, $7x + 6y = 303$

3 a) $r = \sqrt[3]{\dfrac{3V}{4\pi}}$ **b)** 7.84

  c) $c^2 - d^2$ **d)** $4x^2 - 12x + 9$

2 a) $x^2 + 5x - 6$ **b)** $5x + 2$

1 a) +6   **b)** 128   **c)** $6n - 4$

The bare bones of factorisation

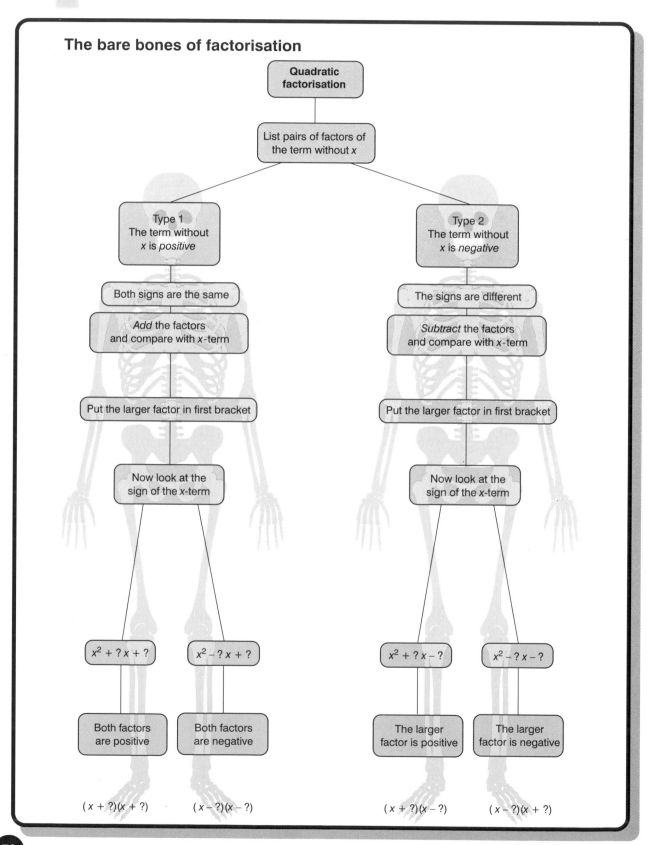

Quadratic factorisation

List pairs of factors of the term without x

Type 1
The term without x is *positive*

Both signs are the same

Add the factors and compare with x-term

Put the larger factor in first bracket

Now look at the sign of the x-term

$x^2 + ? x + ?$

$x^2 - ? x + ?$

Both factors are positive

Both factors are negative

$(x + ?)(x + ?)$

$(x - ?)(x - ?)$

Type 2
The term without x is *negative*

The signs are different

Subtract the factors and compare with x-term

Put the larger factor in first bracket

Now look at the sign of the x-term

$x^2 + ? x - ?$

$x^2 - ? x - ?$

The larger factor is positive

The larger factor is negative

$(x + ?)(x - ?)$

$(x - ?)(x + ?)$

review

How much have you learnt?

Tick off each topic in the list when you are confident you can cope with it.

- Factorise simple algebraic expressions.
- Rearrange formulae.
- Manipulate equations and formulae with powers and roots.
- Solve simultaneous equations algebraically.
- Multiply out brackets.
- Solve inequalities involving powers of x.
- Factorise quadratic equations when the coefficient of x^2 is 1.
- Factorise quadratic equations when the coefficient of x^2 is not 1.
- Factorise the difference of two squares.
- Solve equations by iteration.
- Find the nth terms of sequences.
- Find the next terms in Fibonacci sequences.
- Recognise triangular numbers.

Shapes and constructions

5

Can you scale these mountains?

Regular Hexagon

Mt. Scalene
—all sides and angles are different.

Mt. Isosceles
—two sides and two angles are equal.

Mt. Equilateral
—all sides are the same and all angles are 60°

Regular Pentagon

The Angle Brothers

Acute
$0° < x < 90°$

Obtuse
$90° < x < 180°$

Reflex
$180° < x < 360°$

Could you round up these critters?

Constructing an angle of 60°

Similar triangles

Fixed distance from a point/line/shape

Congruent triangles

Exterior and interior angles

Perpendicular bisector constructing an angle of 90°

preview

By the end of this chapter you will be able to:

- **identify and label angles**

- **recognise the rules for congruency in triangles**

- **identify similar triangles**

- **identify and calculate interior angles, exterior angles**

- **construct a perpendicular bisector of a line, draw a perpendicular from a point to a line**

- **construct an angle of 90°, an angle of 60°, bisect an angle**

- **construct simple loci**

The marked angle at C is made up of two lines AC and CD. To name the angle, you follow the line from A to C to D or vice versa. This is to avoid confusion with the other angle at C running from A to C to B, or vice versa – which is called ∠ACB or ∠BCA.

Triangles

Congruent triangles

Congruent triangles are identical in size and shape, although you may have to flip one over or turn it around for the two to appear to fit together.

Rules for congruency

1   SAS – side, angle, side – two sides and the angle in between are the same

2   AAS – angle, angle, side – two angles and the **corresponding** side are the same

3   SSS – all three sides are the same

4   HRS – hypotenuse, right angle and side are the same

Labelling of angles

The angle marked at C may be called angle ACD or angle DCA. In some books this is written ∠ACD, ∠DCA, AĈD or DĈA.

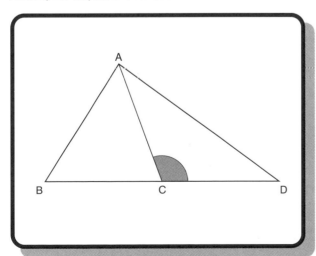

Similar triangles

These triangles have identical angles, but one is an enlargement of the other. Try using X-Direct to find lengths of sides in similar triangles.

Note: The words 'congruent' and 'similar' can describe any group of shapes, but are usually applied to triangles.

Exercise 5.1

1 Z is a point on the side AB of the square ABCD. BX is perpendicular to CZ, and DY is perpendicular to CZ. Prove that △CYD is congruent to △BCX.

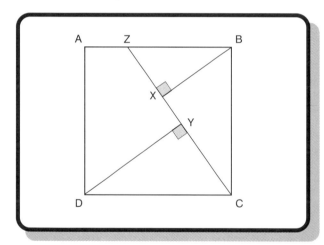

2 In the diagram below, name:
  a) two triangles that are congruent
  b) two triangles that are similar.
  Give reasons for your answer.

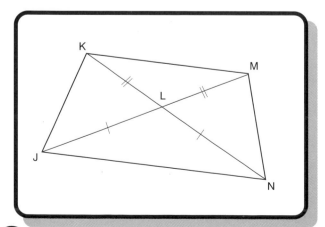

3 △ADE and △BCE are similar. Find:
  a) AE
  b) BE.

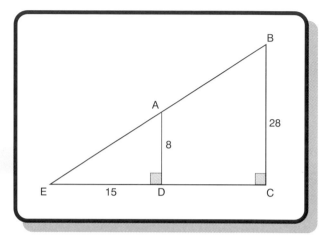

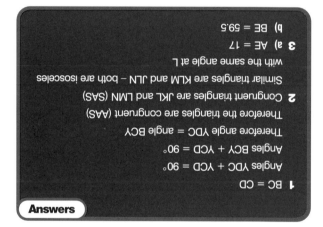

Answers

1 BC = CD
  Angles YDC + YCD = 90°
  Angles BCY + YCD = 90°
  Therefore angle YDC = angle BCY
  Therefore the triangles are congruent (AAS)

2 Congruent triangles are JKL and LMN (SAS)
  Similar triangles are KLM and JLN – both are isosceles with the same angle at L

3 a) AE = 17
  b) BE = 59.5

Exterior angles

An exterior angle of an n-sided regular polygon $= \dfrac{360°}{n}$.

Interior angles

1 Find the exterior angle by using $360° \div n$.

2 As the interior and exterior angles lie on a straight line, they add up to 180°.

Interior angle = 180° – exterior angle

The angle in the centre of a regular polygon is the same as the exterior angle.

Loci and constructions

Whenever drawing loci and constructions, always leave your compass marks on, so that the examiner can tell that you have used the right method.

Loci are lines or curves which join up a group of points. The points are usually described by a rule. The line or curve is called a locus, and 'loci' is the plural form.

Perpendicular bisector

The perpendicu**L**ar bisector is a line which cuts a line in half and is perpendicu**L**ar to it. It is also equidistant (i.e. the same distance) from the end points, A and B.

*Perpendicu**L**ar: at right angles **L** Bisect: cut in half*

Drawing the perpendicular bisector

Example 5.1

The railroad has to run between Bodge City and its rival, Arid Creek. It must be built so that wherever the train stops, it will be equidistant from both cities. Draw a plan of the route of the railroad.

Solution

1 Put the point of your compasses on one end of the line between Arid Creek and Bodge city and open the compasses to a radius which is more than half the length of the line.

2 Using only light pressure, draw an arc either side of the line.

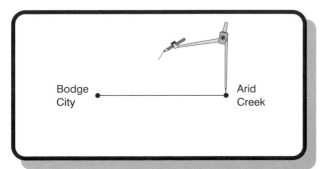

3 Without changing the radius, draw arcs from the other end. Join the two crosses to make the perpendicular bisector.

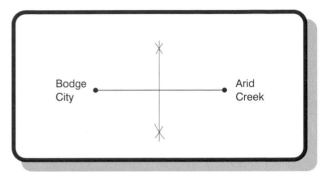

Constructing an angle of 90°

This can be done using the perpendicular bisector method described above.

Constructing an angle of 60°

This is the same as the method used for constructing equilateral triangles.

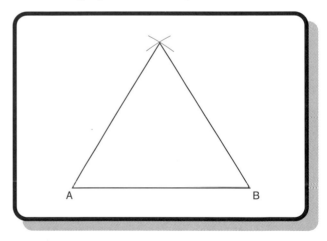

Using any line AB, set your compasses to the same length as AB. Put the point on A and draw an arc, and repeat for B. A line from either end point of AB to this arc makes an angle of 60° with AB.

Do not use loose compasses, and always hold them from the top. The radius must be the same from both ends of the line.

Drawing the shortest distance from a point to a line, or drawing a perpendicular from a line to a point

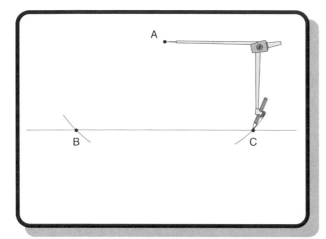

Set your compasses to any length and draw an arc from A, cutting the line twice. The two points of intersection of the arc and line are labelled as B and C. Draw a perpendicular bisector between these points to A. This gives a line, at right angles to BC, that is the shortest distance from BC to A.

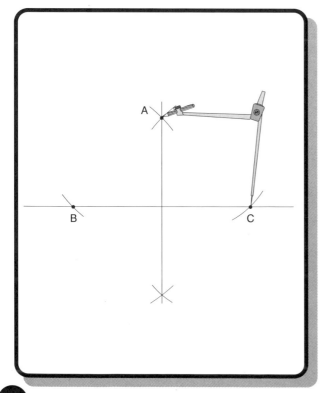

Bisecting an angle

Example 5.2

The Old Mule Express must travel between the Havago and Putemup Trails. The safest path bisects the angle between the trails. Show this on a diagram.

Solution

1   Put the point of the compasses on the point of the angle and make an arc on each arm.

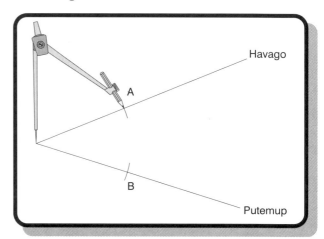

2   Move the point of the compasses to A and B in turn and make a further arc from each. Do not change the radius between drawing from A and drawing from B.

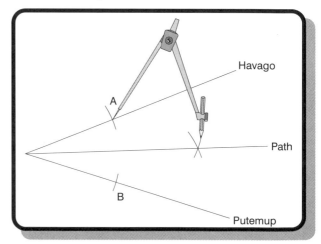

3   Join the cross to the point of the angle to make the bisector of the angle.

Loci

The path of a moving particle that is always a fixed distance from a point will give a circle, with the point at the centre and the distance as the radius.

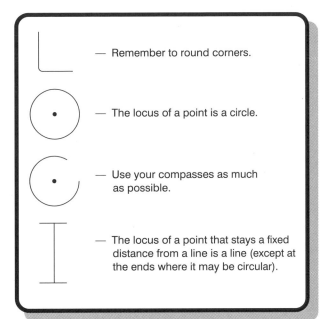

— Remember to round corners.

— The locus of a point is a circle.

— Use your compasses as much as possible.

— The locus of a point that stays a fixed distance from a line is a line (except at the ends where it may be circular).

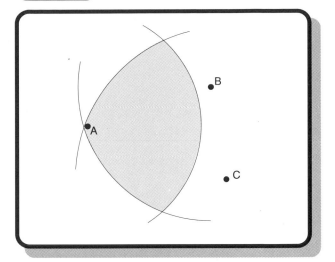

The path of a particle that stays a fixed distance away from a line is a line parallel to it.

Example 5.4

The Putemup Indian Reservation is pictured below. Their smoke signals can be seen up to 2 kilometres away. Using a scale of 1 cm : 1 km, indicate on the diagram below the region in which the smoke signals can be seen.

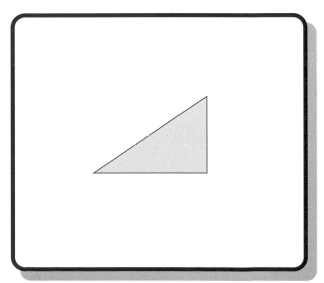

Hint: Be careful to round the corners using compasses.

Example 5.3

Three Indian snipers stand with bows and arrows on three hills, A, B and C. They can fire distances of 90 m, 105 m and 120 m respectively. Shade on the diagram below the most dangerous area, using a scale of 1 cm : 30 m.

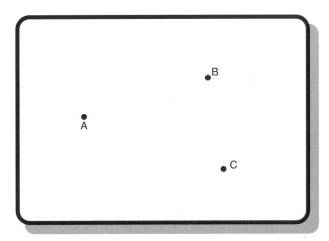

Solution

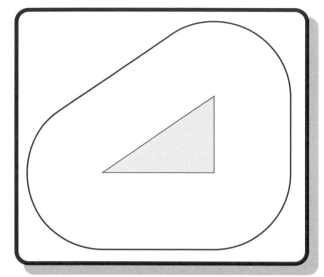

Answers

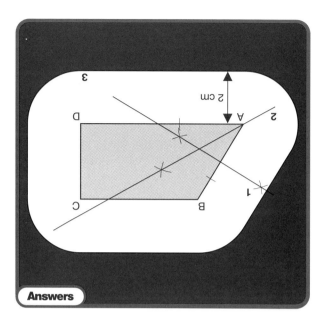

Exercise 5.2

On the diagram below, draw:

1 the perpendicular bisector of AB

2 the locus of the point equidistant from AB and AD

3 the locus of the point 2 cm from ABCD.

Show all your construction lines.

TAKE A BREAK

Take a break before you tackle the exam questions. There has been more than you would think in this chapter.

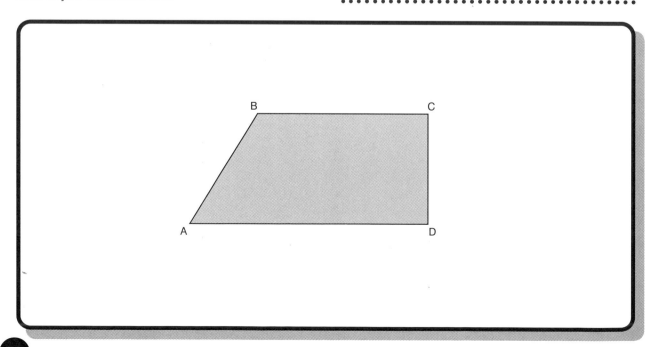

Back to reality!

Exam-type questions 5

None of the diagrams in this section is drawn to scale.

1 All of these triangles are similar. Calculate:
  a) x **b)** y.

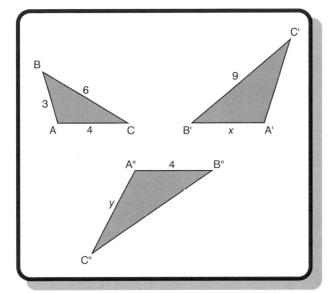

2 A helicopter pad is pictured below. Rotors can extend up to 2.5 m beyond the body of a helicopter. Draw the region around the pad where it would be unsafe to walk, using a scale of 1 cm : 2 m.

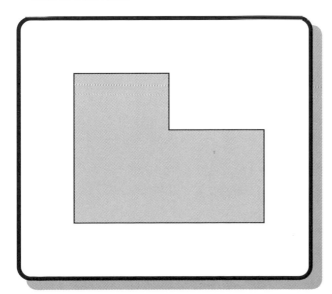

3 a) Explain why triangles PQT and RST are similar.
  b) Find PT.
  c) Find RS.

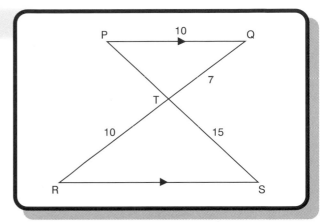

4 ABCDE is a regular pentagon. Find:
  a) ∠EAB   **b)** ∠EBC   **c)** ∠CAB.

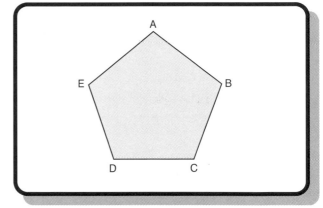

5 Using ruler and compasses only and showing all constructions, draw the shortest line from X to AB.

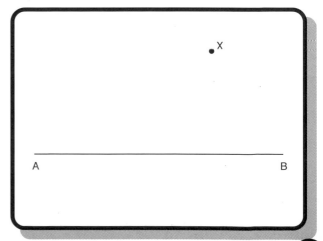

6 Using ruler and compasses only, draw accurately triangle ABC where AB = 4 cm, BC = 5 cm and AC = 6 cm. Mark a point D on BC, such that AD is equidistant from AB and AC. Measure AD. Show all constructions.

7 Using ruler and compasses only, draw a point C above the horizontal line AB so that angle CAB = 90° and angle ABC = 60°. Show all constructions.

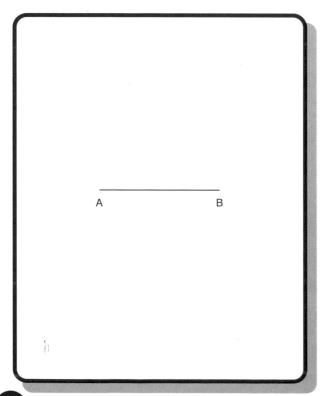

8 The diagram shows part of a regular n-sided polygon.
a) Find the value of r.
b) Hence find the number of sides of the complete polygon.

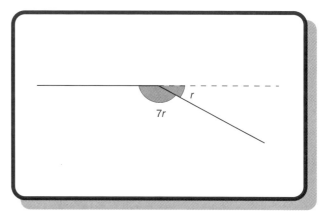

9 State, with reasons, whether the following pairs of triangles are congruent.

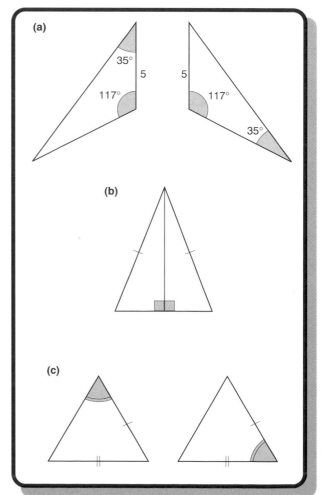

1 a) 4.5   **b)** $5\frac{1}{3}$ or 5.333

2

3 a) PQ and RS are parallel so ∠RTS = ∠PTQ, ∠QPT = ∠RST, ∠PQT = ∠SRT, as all the related angles are identical the triangles are similar.

b) PT = 10.5

c) RS = 14.3

4 a) 108° (using $\frac{360}{n}$ etc.)

b) 72° (angles of quadrilateral EBCD add up to 360°)

c) 36° (triangle EAB is isosceles)

5

6 AD = 4.4 cm

4 cm

6 cm

5 cm

7

8 $r = 22.5°$, $n = 16$

9 a) not congruent (not AAS because the sides are not corresponding)

b) congruent (isosceles triangles can be confirmed by any rule)

c) not congruent (although it appears SAS, the angles do not correspond)

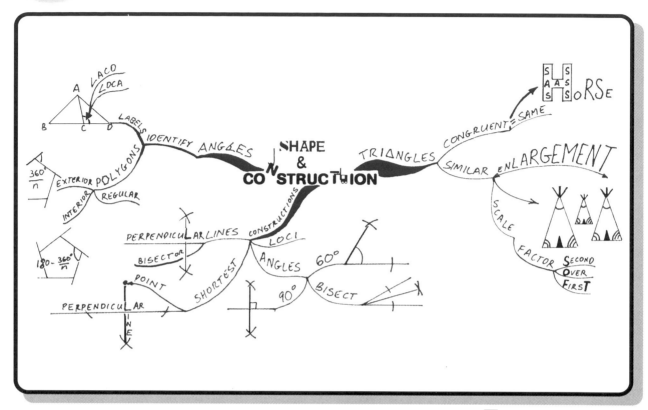

review

How much have you learnt?

Tick off each topic in the list when you are confident you can cope with it.

- Identify and label angles.

- Recognise the rules for congruency in triangles.

- Identify congruent triangles.

- Identify similar triangles.

- Identify interior angles, exterior angles.

- Construct a perpendicular bisector of a line, a perpendicular from a point to a line.

- Construct an angle of 90° an angle of 60°, bisect an angle.

- Construct simple loci.

Pythagoras' theorem and trigonometry

Which of these could you put up?

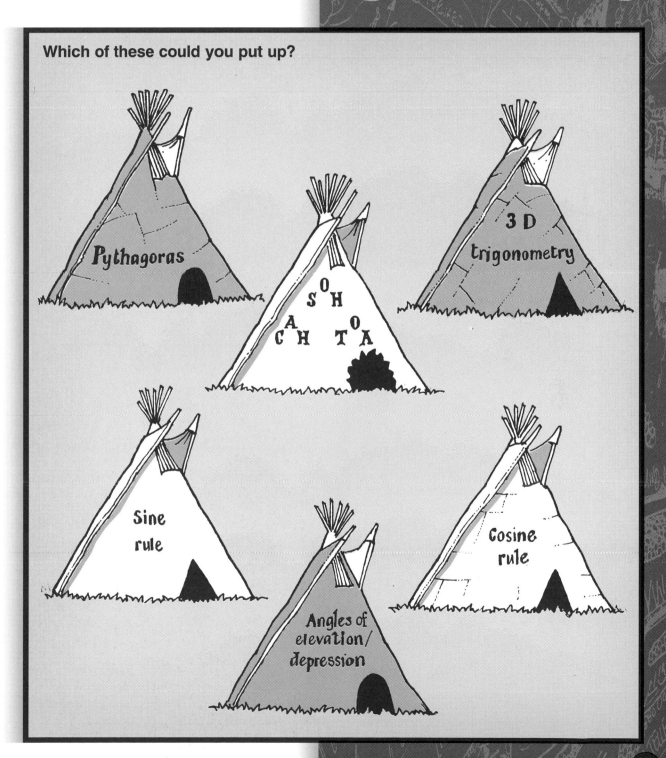

preview

By the end of this chapter you will be able to:

- **solve trigonometric problems involving sine, cosine and tangent of an angle**

- **find missing lengths in a right-angled triangle**

- **solve problems in 3D trigonometry**

- **use the sine rule and cosine rule to solve scalene non-right angled triangles**

Pythagoras – a reminder

$a^2 + b^2 = c^2$

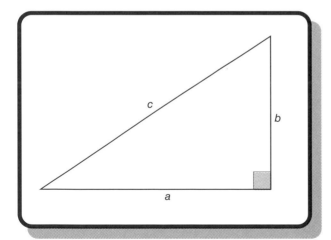

Trigonometry

Always make sure that your calculator is set to degrees before you start, or all your answers will be wrong!

We're suggesting a way of doing trigonometry which is quick on the draw. If you're happy with your own method, skip to Exercise 6.1.

If not, try the following method using SOH CAH TOA.

If you are having trouble remembering SOH CAH TOA, try:

Some Old Hags Can't Always Hide Their Old Age.

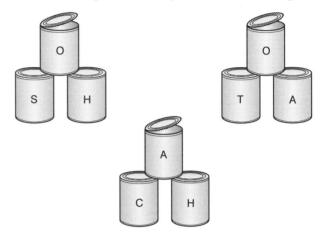

Put your finger over or cross out the relevant letter.

S: $\sin \theta = \dfrac{\text{opp}}{\text{hyp}}$	C: $\cos \theta = \dfrac{\text{adj}}{\text{hyp}}$	T: $\tan \theta = \dfrac{\text{opp}}{\text{adj}}$
O: opp = $\sin \theta \times \text{hyp}$	A: adj = $\cos \theta \times \text{hyp}$	O: opp = $\tan \theta \times \text{adj}$
H: hyp = $\dfrac{\text{opp}}{\sin \theta}$	H: hyp = $\dfrac{\text{adj}}{\cos \theta}$	A: adj = $\dfrac{\text{opp}}{\tan \theta}$

We often use the Greek letter θ (theta) for angles.

Procedure for solving trigonometry problems

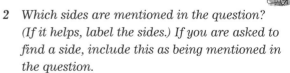

1 *Write out SOH CAH TOA in triplet form.*

2 *Which sides are mentioned in the question? (If it helps, label the sides.) If you are asked to find a side, include this as being mentioned in the question.*

3 *Put your finger over or cross out the letter you want to find, and this will give you the formula.*

This might sound confusing at first, but if you work through the following examples, everything will become clear.

Example 6.1

Find the angle labelled θ in the triangle below.

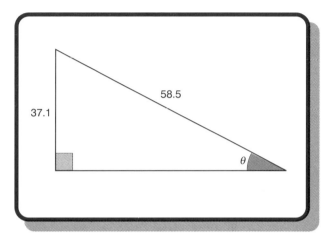

Solution

This question includes the opposite (opp) and hypotenuse (hyp), so use SOH. Drawing out the triplet gives:

$$\sin \theta = \frac{\text{opp}}{\text{hyp}} = \frac{37.1}{58.5}$$

$$\sin \theta = 0.6342$$

To find the angle, you need its inverse (in this case, inverse sin or $\sin^{-1}$).

$$\theta = \sin^{-1}(0.6342)$$

$$= 39.4° \text{ correct to 1 d.p.}$$

If you are getting an Error sign on your calculator or a ridiculous answer, you are probably not pressing ▢= before you press INV SIN , COS or TAN . Also, some calculators require you to press ▢= at the end, or use brackets, so it's a good idea to find out in good time how yours works. If you still can't find out where you went wrong, check that your calculator is set on degrees!

Example 6.2

Find the length labelled x in the triangle below.

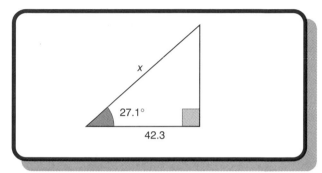

Solution

Using

$$\text{hyp} = \frac{\text{adj}}{\cos \theta}$$

$$x = \frac{42.3}{\cos 27.1°}$$

$$x = 47.5 \text{ (correct to 1 d.p.)}$$

What about isosceles triangles?

Meet Tom O'Hourke, with his big chopper
Tom O'Hourke stands them on their odd side and chops vertically downwards, to give the perpendicular bisector.

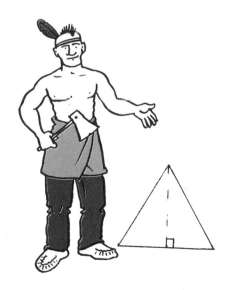

Angles of elevation and depression

Angles of **elevation** and **depression** must be measured from the horizontal. You look at the horizon and move your head up for an angle of elevation or down for an angle of depression.

3D trigonometry

The secret of working in 3D is to find a right-angled triangle. If this is not obvious, draw a line from the starting point to the peak or top point of the 'solid' shape. From there, draw another line vertically down, and join the point where it hits the ground to your starting point. You should now have a right-angled triangle. You may need to use Pythagoras' theorem as well as trigonometry.

The most usual questions involve pyramids, wedges or cuboids.

Remember, when working with 3D coordinates, they are given in the order (x, y, z). Be careful with the axes in the diagrams you are given. They may not be labelled in the order you expect.

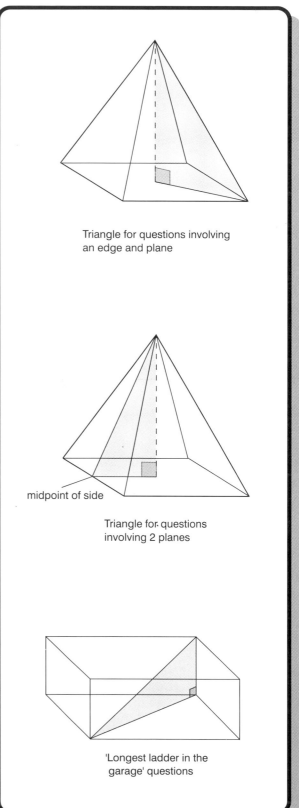

Triangle for questions involving an edge and plane

midpoint of side

Triangle for questions involving 2 planes

'Longest ladder in the garage' questions

Example 6.3

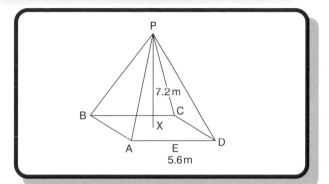

The diagram shows a square-based pyramid. The point P is directly above the centre of the square, X. E is the midpoint of AD. AD = 5.6 m and PX = 7.2 m.

a) Find the angle PDX.

b) Find the length of PD.

c) Find the angle PEX.

Solution

a) DX = 3.96 by Pythagoras' theorem.
∠PDX = inverse tan(7.2 ÷ 3.96) = 61.2°

b) PD = 8.2 m (Use △PXD)

c) ∠PEX = inverse tan(7.2 ÷ 2.8) = 68.7°

Example 6.4

Old Mary stores timber in a cuboid-shaped barn. Find the longest possible length of timber that would fit in the barn.

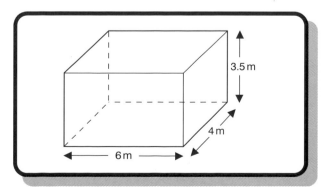

Solution

The longest piece of timber would go from a vertex at the bottom to a diagonally opposite vertex at the top.

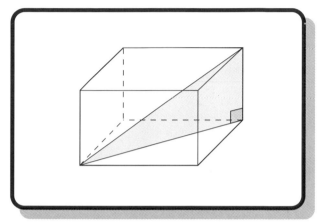

Find the length of the diagonal on the base:
$\sqrt{6^2 + 4^2} = 7.2$ m

Length of the longest piece of timber:
$\sqrt{7.2^2 + 3.5^2} = 8.0$ m

Trigonometry for non-right angled scalene triangles

Scalene triangles have no sides equal. There are two rules for non-right angled scalene triangles: the sine and the cosine rules. These formulae are usually given on the *Information and formulae sheet.*

How do I know which rule to use?

If there is an angle and its opposite side given in the question, use the sine rule. Otherwise use the cosine rule.

The sine rule

This rule is used when the question involves two angles and two lengths.

This version of the formula is easier to use for finding angles:

$$\frac{\sin A}{a} = \frac{\sin B}{b} = \frac{\sin C}{c}$$

and this one is easier for finding lengths:

$$\frac{a}{\sin A} = \frac{b}{\sin B} = \frac{c}{\sin C}$$

6

The cosine rule

This rule applies when you are working with three lengths and one angle.

To find length a: $a^2 = b^2 + c^2 - 2bc \cos A$

To find angle A: $\cos A = \dfrac{b^2 + c^2 - a^2}{2bc}$

and use **INV** **COS** to find the angle.

Can you work out the formulae for sides b and c, and for angles B and C?

Bearings – a summary

1 Always use three-figure numbers.

2 Always start from the North and go clockwise.

Exercise 6.1

1 Using the triangle below, find:
  a) BD   **b)** CD.

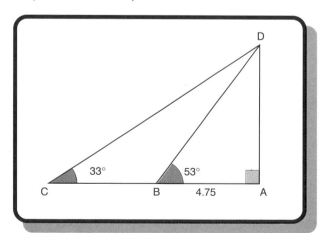

2 Chief Wairameye is lost. He walks 6.2 km on a bearing of 111°. He then changes direction and walks 5.9 km on a bearing of 348°. Using trigonometry, find his distance (to the nearest 0.1 kilometre) and the bearing from his original point (to the nearest degree).

3 Pocafinga stands at a point C at the top of a vertical cliff. Lowawatha in a canoe at B sees Pocafinga at C, a distance of 210 m away. Lowawatha is 156 m from the base of the cliff. What is the angle of depression of Lowawatha from Pocafinga?

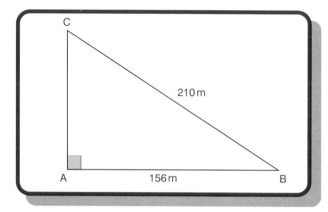

4 In the diagram below find:
  a) the length marked x **b)** the angle y.

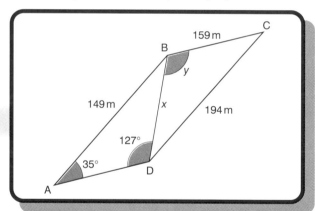

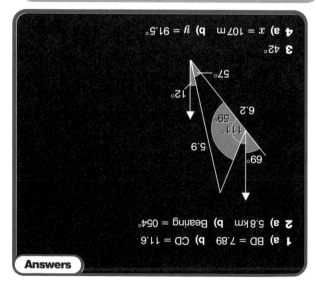

Answers

4 a) $x = 107\,\text{m}$ **b)** $y = 91.5°$

3 42°

2 a) 5.8 km   **b)** Bearing = 054°

1 a) BD = 7.89   **b)** CD = 11.6

TAKE A BREAK

Still bearing up? Take a break before you check out the rest of this chapter. You could draw your own mind map to help you keep track of all that trig.

Noses to the grindstone!

Exam-type questions 6

1 Find x in the following.

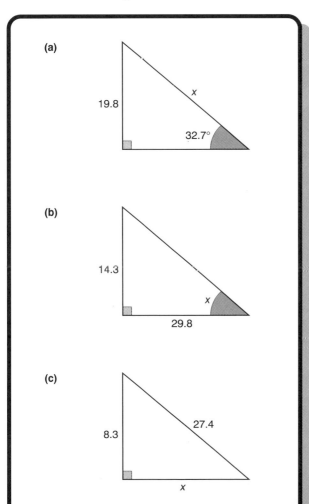

(a)

19.8

x

32.7°

(b)

14.3

x

29.8

(c)

8.3

27.4

x

2 Is the angle at B a right angle, acute or obtuse?

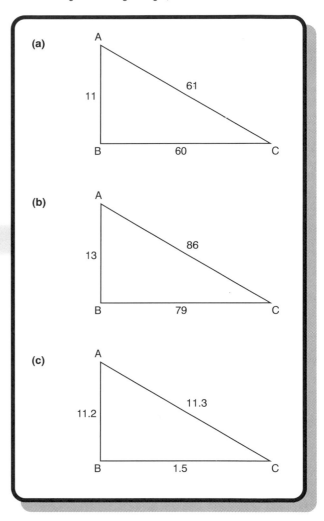

(a)

A

11

61

B   60   C

(b)

A

13

86

B   79   C

(c)

A

11.2

11.3

B   1.5   C

3 a) What is the name given to this type of triangle?

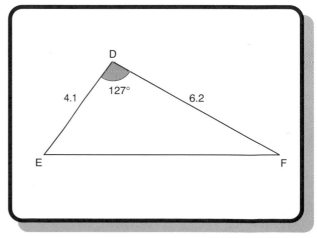

D

4.1   127°   6.2

E   F

b) Find EF.

89

4 A is a point at the top of a vertical cliff 20 m high. The angle of depression from A to a point C is 57°. Calculate BC.

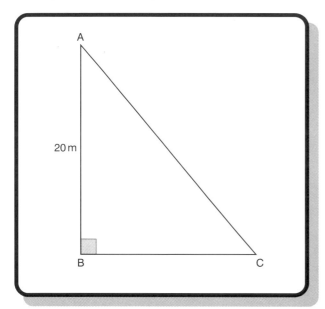

5 A, B and C are three towers. B is on a bearing of 250° from C and 8 km away from it. C is on a bearing of 051° and 30 km from A.
a) Calculate AB.
b) Calculate the bearing of B from A.
c) Taking 1 km to equal $\frac{5}{8}$ mile give the distance AB in miles.

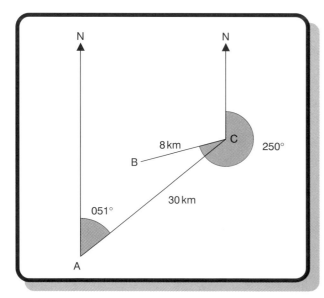

6 The diagram shows a cuboid. The coordinates of A are (6, 0, 0) and of F are (6, 3, 4). Find:
a) the coordinates of the points G and C
b) the length OB
c) the length OF.

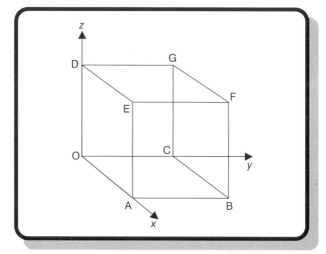

7 In the triangle PQS, find:
a) PS   **b)** RQ   **c)** ∠RPQ.

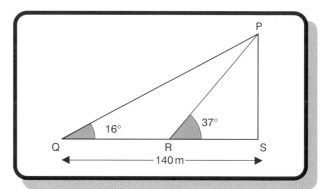

8 In the triangle JKL, find:
a) JL   **b)** KL   **c)** the area of triangle JKL.

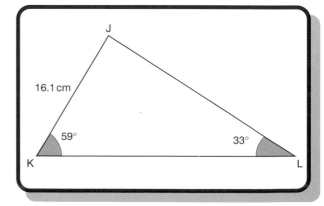

9 A tanker is at a bearing of 117° from a port, and a lighthouse is at a bearing of 261° from the tanker and 197° from the port. The distance of the lighthouse from the port is 562 m. Find:
a) angle PTL
b) the distance of the lighthouse from the tanker.

11 AO represents a tree 10.6 m tall. Two people standing at B and C respectively are looking at the top of the tree. The angle of elevation from B to the top of the tree is 35° and from C is 52°. Find:
a) OB   **b)** OC   **c)** BC.

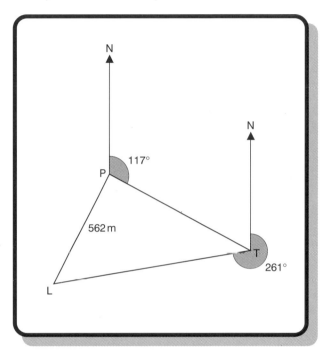

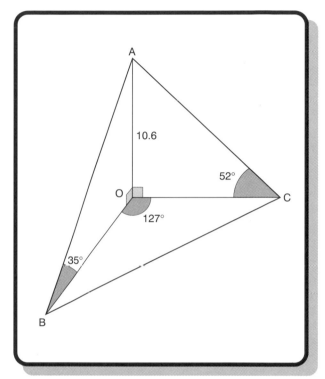

10 In the triangle ABC, calculate:
a) the perpendicular height from C to AB produced
b) the area of triangle ABC
c) the length of BC.

12 The diagram shows a square-based pyramid with a vertical height AX of 22.6 cm and a base of side 15 cm. Find:
a) the length of AD
b) angle ADX
c) the angle between the plane ABE and the base.

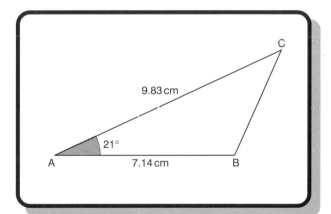

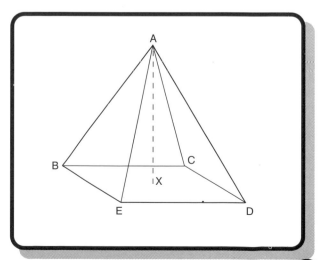

Answers

1 a) 36.7 **b)** 26° **c)** 26.1

2 a) 90° **b)** obtuse **c)** 90°

3 a) non-right angled scalene (i.e. all 3 sides different lengths)
b) 9.3 to 1 d.p.

4 (Remember that the angles of depression are measured from the horizontal.) 13 m

5 a) 22.6 km **b)** 044° **c)** 14.1 miles

6 a) G = (0, 3, 4), C = (0, 3, 0)
b) OB = 6.7
c) OF = 7.8

7 a) 40.14
b) RQ = 140 − 53.3 = 86.7 (RS = 53.3)
c) 21° (It is easier to use the fact that the angles of a triangle add to 180°.)

8 a) 25.3 cm **b)** 29.5 cm **c)** 204 cm²

9 a) 36° **b)** 941.6 m

10 a) 3.52 cm
b) 12.6 cm²
c) 4.07 cm

11 a) 15.14 m **b)** 8.28 m **c)** 21.2 m

12 a) 24.97 (using Pythagoras' theorem, X is the midpoint of BD, XD = 10.6)
b) 65° to the nearest degree
c) inverse tan (22.6 ÷ 7.5) = 72° to the nearest degree

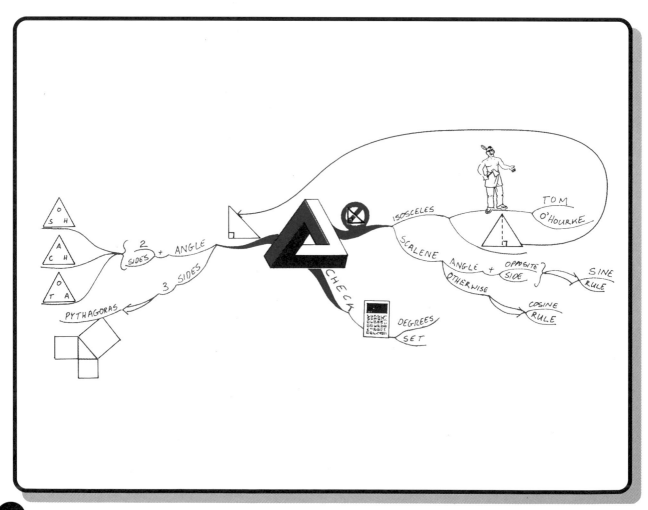

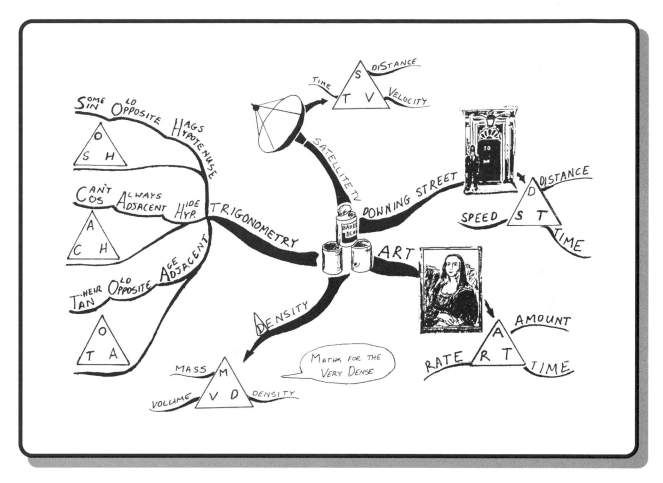

review

How much have you learnt?

Tick off each topic in the list when you are confident you can cope with it.

- Solve trigonometric problems involving sine, cosine and tangent of an angle.

- Find missing lengths in a right-angled triangle.

- Solve problems in 3D trigonometry.

- Use the sine rule and cosine rule to solve scalene non-right angled triangles

Length, area and volume

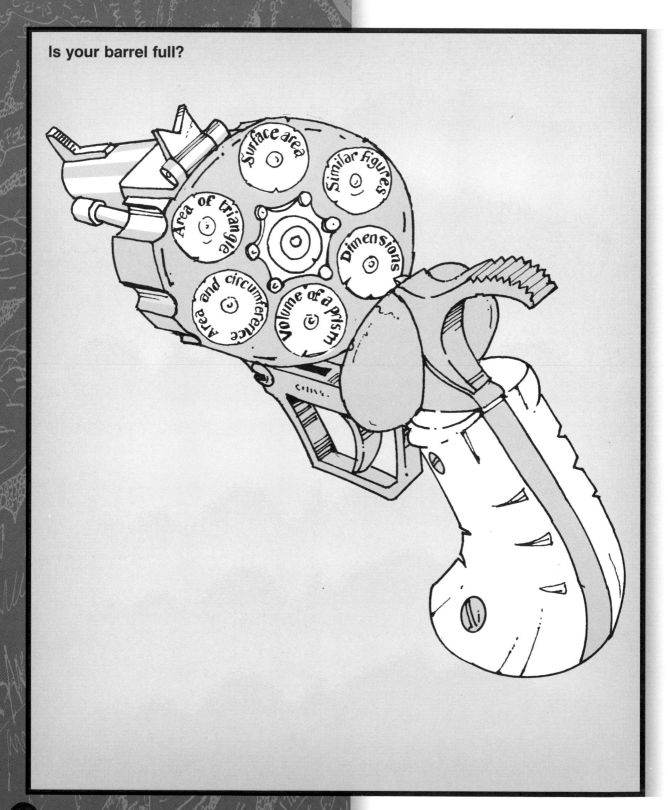

7

Is your barrel full?

Surface area

Similar figures

Area of triangle

Dimensions

Area and circumference

Volume of a prism

preview

By the end of this chapter you will be able to:

- calculate the area of a triangle

- calculate the area and circumference of a circle

- find the surface area of 3D shapes

- find the volume of a prism

- identify the dimensions in an expression and check that the quantity is valid

- calculate scale factors for area and volume, given a linear scale factor for similar shapes

Area

Area of a triangle

In a triangle, if you know the base and perpendicular height (or the equivalent turned around), you can use:

area of a triangle = $\frac{1}{2} \times$ base $\times$ height

If not, you must use:

area = $\frac{1}{2}ab\sin C$

This will probably be on your *Information and formulae sheet*.

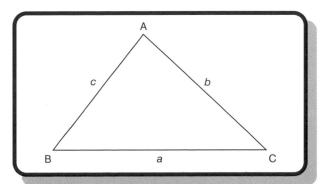

Area and circumference of a circle

πr *squarea gives you the area*, πr^2

$2\pi r$ *(or πd) gives the circumference.*

Surface area of 3D shapes

Imagine your 3D shape opened out into a net, then describe the shape of each of the pieces. By finding the areas of these pieces and adding them, you will find the total surface area of the shape.

For example, a solid cylinder
= 2 circles + 1 rectangle = $2\pi r^2 + 2\pi rh$

Check if the hollow cylinder or cuboid has a lid.

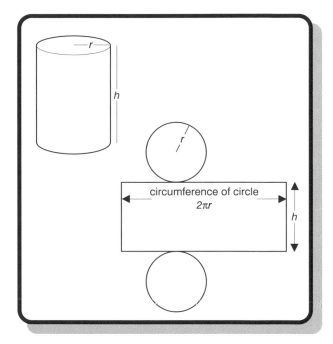

Volume

Volume of a prism (sometimes called a right prism)

A prism is a 3D shape which you can cut into identical slices.

For example, if you slice a cylinder, each piece is a circle.

The name given to the shape of each slice is the **cross-section**.

The volume of a prism is area of cross-section × length.

V stands for volume. The word 'volume' is usually used, but occasionally you may be asked for capacity.

A stands for the area of the cross-section.

L stands for length.
But remember you may not be asked for the length. Instead you may be asked for a width, depth, height or thickness.

Dimensions

In questions on dimensions you will be given expressions and asked whether they relate to length, area or volume or are impossibilities.

These questions are easier to understand if you work in a basic unit. For convenience, we shall use cm, cm^2 or cm^3 in the following way.

Length	cm	1 dimension
Area	cm^2	2 dimensions
Volume	cm^3	3 dimensions

NB Any measurement of length, area or volume follows the same pattern.

Rule 1 – adding like with like
- length + length = length (or perimeter)
  cm + cm = cm

- area + area = area
  $cm^2 + cm^2 = cm^2$

- volume + volume = volume
  $cm^3 + cm^3 = cm^3$

Rule 2 – multiplication of dimensions
Use TIP (Times Indices Plus)

- length × length = area
  $cm^1 \times cm^1 = cm^2$

- length × length × length = volume
  $cm^1 \times cm^1 \times cm^1 = cm^3$

- area × length = volume
  $cm^2 \times cm^1 = cm^3$

Rule 3 – division of dimensions
Use DIM (Divide Indices Minus)

- volume ÷ area = length
  $cm^3 \div cm^2 = cm^1$

- volume ÷ length = area
  $cm^3 \div cm^1 = cm^2$

Rule 4 – adding or subtracting different dimensions gives a nonsense result

For example   length + area = nonsense!

                   volume + area = nonsense!

If possible work with the expressions alone. The diagrams are often confusing and unnecessary.

Meet Sure Shot Stan – the dimensions man

Follow this infallible method!

1 Sure Shot Stan shoots out all the whole numbers, fractions and π s.

2 Each remaining letter represents a dimension. Change each of them to cm^1, cm^2 or cm^3 as appropriate.

3 Simplify the expression, following the four rules.

4 Look at your final answer and decide whether it represents length, area, volume or nonsense.

Example 7.1

The letters p, q and r represent lengths. Are the following formulae for length, area, volume or none of these?

a) $\pi p^2 q - 2r^2$ **b)** $\frac{4}{3}\pi pqr$ **c)** $p\sqrt{q^2 - r^2}$

d) $\pi p(2q + r)$ **e)** $\dfrac{4p^3}{qr}$

Solution

Step 1: Sure Shot Stan (the dimensions man) shoots out all numbers (this includes π and fractions).

a) $\pi p^2 q - 2r^2$

b) $\frac{4}{3}\pi pqr$

c) $p\sqrt{q^2 - r^2}$

d) $\pi p(2q + r)$

e) $\dfrac{4p^3}{qr}$

Steps 2 to 4: He converts all lengths to cm, areas to cm² and volumes to cm³ and combines them.

a) $p^2q - r^2 = \text{cm}^2\text{cm} - \text{cm}^2 = \text{cm}^3 - \text{cm}^2$
        $= \text{nonsense!}$

b) $pqr = \text{cm} \times \text{cm} \times \text{cm} = \text{cm}^3 = \text{volume}$

c) $p\sqrt{q^2 - r^2} = \text{cm}\sqrt{\text{cm}^2 - \text{cm}^2} = \text{cm}\sqrt{\text{cm}^2} = \text{cm} \times \text{cm}$
        $= \text{cm}^2 = \text{area}$

d) $p(q + r) = \text{cm}(\text{cm} + \text{cm}) = \text{cm} \times \text{cm} = \text{cm}^2$
        $= \text{area}$

e) $\dfrac{p^3}{qr} = \text{cm}^3 \div \text{cm}^2 = \text{cm} = \text{length}$

Exercise 7.1

The letters p, q and r represent lengths. Decide whether the following are lengths, areas, volumes or none of these.

1 $4\pi r^2 + r\sqrt{p^2 + q^2}$ **2** $\dfrac{2p^2}{\pi r}$ **3** $6pr^2 - \pi q^2 r$

4 $2pq + 3r$ **5** $\sqrt{p^2 + q^2 + qr}$ **6** $\dfrac{\pi pq^2}{6r}$

Answers

1 area
2 length
3 volume
4 none of these
5 length
6 area

TAKE A BREAK

Take a break and take stock, before you go on to scale factors.

Length, area and volume scale factors for similar figures

If two figures are similar, one is an exact enlargement of the other. The word 'enlargement' can also be applied to shapes becoming smaller.

To calculate the volume scale factor when you have an area scale factor (and vice versa) you need to find the length scale factor first.

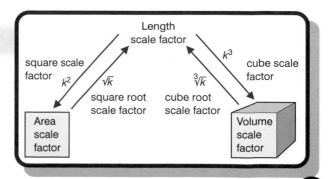

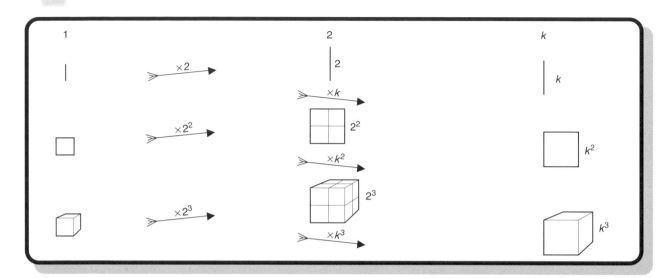

If one object has length 2 times as big as another, then the area will be 2^2 times as big and the volume 2^3 times as big.

If one object has length k times as big as another, then the area will be k^2 times as big and the volume k^3 times as big.

Similar shapes

If the areas are in the ratio $k : 1$, then the lengths are in the ratio $\sqrt{k} : 1$ (or $k^{\frac{1}{2}} : 1$).

If the volumes are in the ratio $k : 1$, then the lengths are in the ratio $\sqrt[3]{k} : 1$ (or $k^{\frac{1}{3}} : 1$).

Example 7.2

The Kanvas City Grocery Store sells Trail Ale in similar bottles. The height of the smaller bottle is 15 cm and the height of the larger bottle is 30 cm. If the smaller bottle holds 0.75 litres, how much does the larger hold?

Solution

Step 1: Firstly find the scale factor –
Second Over FirsT = $30 \div 15 = 2$

Step 2: Volume scale factor = $k^3 = 2^3 = 8$

So the larger bottle holds 8 times as much as the smaller bottle.

Volume = $8 \times 0.75 = 6$ litres

Example 7.3

Chief Sitting Duck insists that the dimensions of his tepee are 2.5 times those of his son's tepee. If his son's tepee has a base area of $16\,\text{m}^2$ and a volume of $45\,\text{m}^3$, evaluate the area and volume of Sitting Duck's tepee.

Solution

Area = $2.5^2 \times 16 = 100\,\text{m}^2$

Volume = $2.5^3 \times 45 = 703\,\text{m}^3$

Example 7.4

Lowawatha was given special dispensation by the Chief to have a tepee that was similar to the Chief's, but with lengths 0.8 of the lengths of the Chief's. Using the results above, work out the area and volume of Lowawatha's tepee.

Solution

Area = $0.8^2 \times 100$
  = $64\,\text{m}^2$

Volume = $0.8^3 \times 703$
  = $360\,\text{m}^3$

Example 7.5

The Havago and Putemup tribes have similar blankets. The area of the Havago's blanket is 296.45 m² and the area of the Putemup's blanket is 24.2 m².

a) Find the area scale factor of the enlargement from Havago to Putemup.

b) If the length of the Havago blanket is 26.25 m, find the length of the Putemup blanket.

Solution

a) Area scale factor = 24.2 ÷ 296.45 = 0.0816

b) Length scale factor = $\sqrt{0.0816}$ = 0.286

Length = 26.25 × $\sqrt{0.0816}$ = 7.5 m

Example 7.6

Shady Deals Finance Co. have similar windows in their clerk's office and shop front. The areas of the windows are 1.4 m² and 8.75 m² respectively. If the length of the office window is 80 cm, what would be the corresponding length of the shop window?

Solution

Area scale factor = 8.75 ÷ 1.4 = 6.25

Length = 0.80 × $\sqrt{6.25}$ = 2 m

Example 7.7

Hugely High Hal and Vertically Challenged Chas have similar water flasks in their saddle bags. Hal's holds 6 litres and Chas's holds 2.2 litres. If Hal's flask is 35 cm high, find the height of Chas's.

Solution

Volume scale factor = 2.2 ÷ 6 = 0.367

Length scale factor = $\sqrt[3]{0.367}$ = 0.716

Height of Chas's flask = 35 × 0.716 = 25 cm

Exercise 7.2

1 Chief Wairameye is always getting lost. He insists that his totem pole is similar to the next tribe's totem pole with a length scale factor of 1.75, so that he can always find his way home.
   a) If his neighbour's totem pole is 8.5 m high, find the height of Chief Wairameye's totem pole.
   b) If the smaller pole uses 6.7 m³ of wood, find the volume of Chief Wairameye's totem pole.

2 In Bodge City's Jail, the Sheriff decreed that the length and width of his office should be 3.7 times that of the cell. If the area of the cell is 10.1 m², find the area demanded by the Sheriff.

3 Arid Creek's Grocery Store sells Weevil's Wundarusks in similar packets. Large packets are 24 cm long and small packets are 15 cm long. If large packets weigh 450 g, find how much the smaller packet weighs, to the nearest gram.

4 Kanvas City's Marshal ordered a Wanted poster (area 600 cm²) of the notorious Kid Vicious. When it arrived, it was found to be similar but of area 864 cm².
   a) What was the area scale factor?
   b) What was the linear scale factor?
   c) If the length ordered was 30 cm, what was the length of the poster delivered?

5 The Last Burp Saloon stores Drooper's Brew in a large barrel holding 600 litres. It is sold to customers in similar barrels which hold 5 litres. If the height of the large barrel is 1.6 m, find the height of the smaller barrel.

Answers

5 0.32 m or 32 cm
4 a) 1.44 **b)** 1.2 **c)** 36 cm
3 110 g
2 138.3 m²
1 a) 14.9 m **b)** 35.9 m³

TAKE A BREAK

Take a break. By now your own mind maps should be shaping up well. Add what you have learnt in this chapter.

Out of the frying pan …

Exam-type questions 7

1 a, b and c are lengths. State whether each of the following formulae represents a length, area, volume or none of these.

a) $\frac{1}{4}\pi a^2 b + b^3$ **b)** $\pi ab - \frac{3}{4}b^3$

c) $\sqrt{b^2 + c^2}$ **d)** $b^3 \div a$

e) $a(b^2 + \pi c^2)$ **f)** $\dfrac{\pi a^2 b}{c^2}$

2 A scoop, illustrated below, is in the form of a prism. The shaded end is a trapezium. Find the volume of the scoop.

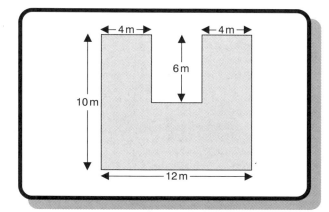

3 The diagram represents a flower bed.

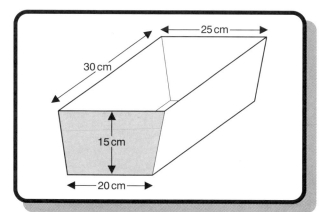

a) Find its perimeter.
b) Find its area.
c) If it is covered by compost to a depth of 15 cm, give the volume of compost in cubic metres.

4 A cylindrical glass, full of water, has volume 186.5 cm³. If its diameter is 5 cm, how deep is the water?

5 State, with a reason, whether the following pairs of triangles are definitely congruent.

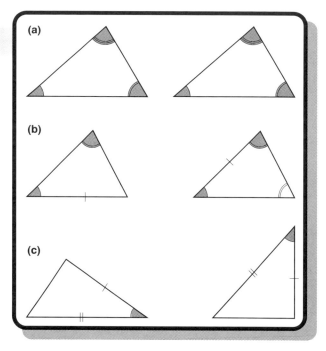

6 Two containers are similar. The areas of their bases are 5.3 m² and 33.125 m². If the height of the smaller is 4.8 m find the height of the larger.

7 Two triangular-based prisms are similar. The smaller has a volume of 648 cm³ and a cross-sectional area of 54 cm². If the volume of the larger prism is 17 496 cm³, find the length of the larger.

8 A map is drawn to the scale of 1 : 25 000. A field has an area on the map of 6 cm². What is its actual area, in km²?

9 Two triangles are similar. The area of triangle A is 4 cm² and the area of triangle B is 9 cm². Write the ratio of areas in the form A : B, and that of their sides in the same form.

10 A cuboid with a volume 2.475 litres is filled with water. The contents are poured into a cylinder of radius 6 cm.
a) What would be the depth of the water in the cylinder?
b) The contents are then poured into a second cylindrical vessel, filling it completely. If the height of this vessel is 18.2 cm, find the base radius.

11 The area of a plate is 16.5 cm². Find its diameter.

12 A model of a boat is built to a scale of 1 : 60. If the real boat is 17.2 m long, find the length of the model in centimetres, correct to one decimal place.

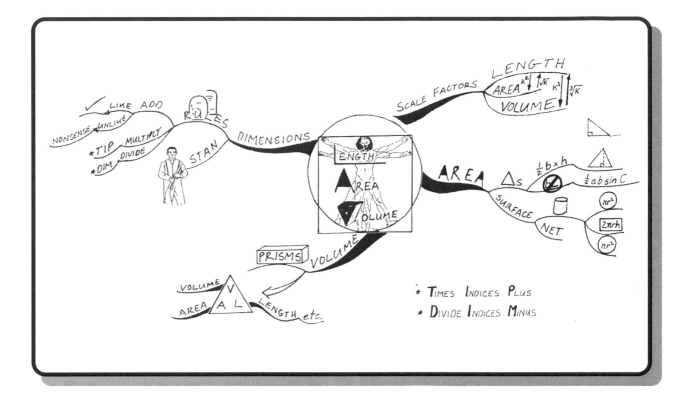

* TIMES INDICES PLUS
* DIVIDE INDICES MINUS

1 a) volume **b)** none **c)** length **d)** area
  e) volume **f)** length
2 volume = 10 125 cm³
3 a) 56 m **b)** 96 m² **c)** 14.4 m³ (15 cm = 0.15 m)
4 9.5 cm
5 a) similar, not necessarily congruent
  b) not necessarily congruent as the given sides do
      not correspond
  c) congruent (SAS)
6 12 m
      33.125 ÷ 5.3 = 6.25 = area scale factor; √6.25 = 2.5.
7 17 496 ÷ 648 = 27 = volume scale factor; ³√27 = 3;
      648 ÷ 54 = 12 (length of smaller prism); length of
      larger prism = 12 × 3 = 36 cm
8 length = 1 : 25 000, area = 1² : 25 000²
      = 1 : 625 000 000
      field area = 6 × 625 000 000 = 3 750 000 000 cm²
      = 375 000 m² = 0.375 km²
9 Area 4 : 9 = 1 : 2.25, sides 2 : 3 = 1 : 1.5
10 a) 21.9 m **b)** 6.6 cm
11 diameter = 4.6 cm (remember 2r)
12 28.7 cm

review

How much have you learnt?

**Tick off each topic in the list when you
are confident you can cope with it.**

◯ Calculate the area of a triangle.

◯ Calculate the area and circumference of a
   circle.

◯ Find the surface area of 3D shapes.

◯ Find the volume of a prism.

◯ Identify the dimensions in an expression
   and check that the quantity is valid.

◯ Calculate scale factors for area and
   volume, given a linear scale factor for
   similar shapes.

Circles

A circle round up

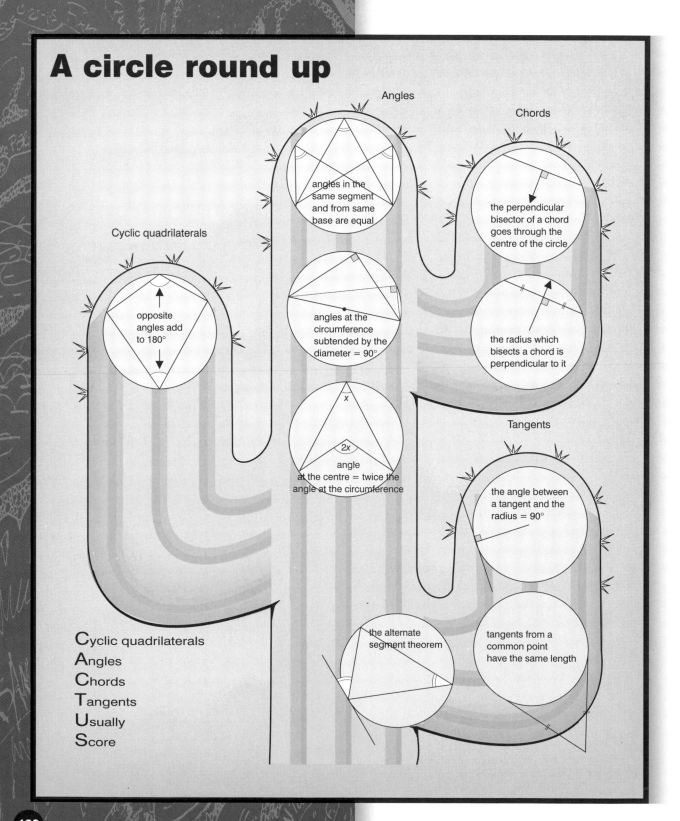

Angles

angles in the same segment and from same base are equal

angles at the circumference subtended by the diameter = 90°

x

$2x$

angle at the centre = twice the angle at the circumference

Chords

the perpendicular bisector of a chord goes through the centre of the circle

the radius which bisects a chord is perpendicular to it

Cyclic quadrilaterals

opposite angles add to 180°

Tangents

the angle between a tangent and the radius = 90°

the alternate segment theorem

tangents from a common point have the same length

Cyclic quadrilaterals
Angles
Chords
Tangents
Usually
Score

preview

- **recognise cyclic quadrilaterals**

- **use the rules applying to cyclic quadrilaterals**

- **recognise angles, chords and tangents in circles**

- **use the basic rules that apply to angles, chords and tangents in circles**

- **find the area of a sector of a circle**

- **find the length of an arc of a circle**

- **find the area of a segment of a circle**

Do any of these arrows leave you in a quiver?

The rules for circles

Cyclic quadrilaterals

1   Opposite angles add up to 180°.

Angles

1   Angles in the same segment and from the same base are equal.

2   The angle subtended at the circumference by the diameter is 90°.

3   The angle subtended by an arc at the centre is twice the angle subtended by the same arc at the circumference.

Chords

1   The perpendicular bisector of a chord passes through the centre of a circle.

2   If the radius passes through the midpoint of a chord then the lines are perpendicular.

Tangents

1   The angle between a tangent and a radius is 90°.

2   Tangents from a common point have the same length.

3   The alternate segment theorem – the angle between a tangent and a chord is equal to the angle subtended by that chord in the alternate segment.

It's much easier to look at the CACTus diagram for this.

Note the number of rules under each of the above headings. When you meet a question of this type, use the rules to fill in as much information as you can. Then, looking back at the question you may find you have already answered it!

The area of a sector

If the area of a circle is πr^2 then:

- the area of a 1° sector is $\dfrac{\pi r^2}{360}$

- the area of a $\theta°$ sector is $\theta \times \dfrac{\pi r^2}{360}$

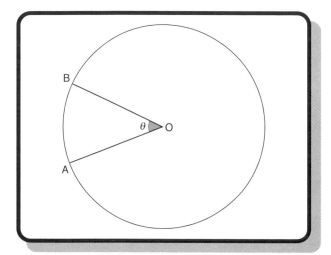

Arc length

If the circumference of a circle is $2\pi r$ then:

- an arc length which subtends an angle of 1° at the centre has length $\dfrac{2\pi r}{360}$

- an arc length which subtends an angle of $\theta°$ at the centre has length $\theta \times \dfrac{2\pi r}{360}$

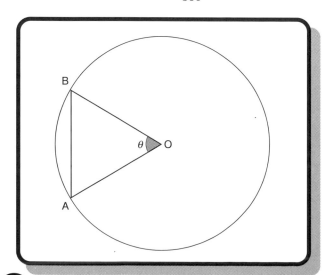

Area of a segment

area of a segment = area of the sector – area of triangle

It is easier to use the formula for the area of any triangle as $\frac{1}{2}ab\sin C$.

Example 8.1

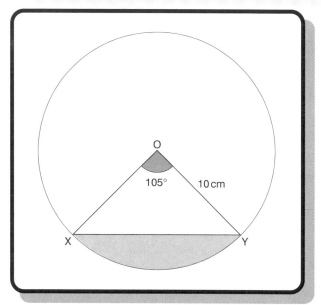

In the circle above, find:

a) the minor arc XY   b) the major arc XY

c) the area of sector OXY   d) the area of △OXY

e) the area of the shaded segment.

Solution

a) Arc length $= \theta \times \dfrac{2\pi r}{360} = 18.3\,\text{cm}$

b) Major arc XY (this is the long way round from
   X to Y) $= \theta \times \dfrac{2\pi r}{360} = 44.5\,\text{cm}$

   using $\theta = 360° - 105° = 255°$

c) Area of sector $= \theta \times \dfrac{\pi r^2}{360} = 91.6\,\text{cm}^2$

d) Area of △OXY $= \frac{1}{2}ab\sin C = 48.3\,\text{cm}^2$

e) Area of shaded segment $= 91.6 - 48.3 = 43.3\,\text{cm}^2$

TAKE A BREAK

Mind in a spin? Take a break and prepare for the exam questions.

Crunch time

Exam-type questions 8

1 JL and KL are tangents to the circle centred at O. M is a point on the circumference of this circle. Find the angles a, b and c.

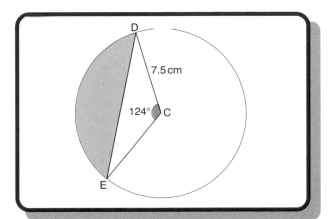

2 DE is a chord of a circle centred at C, with a radius of 7.5 cm. Angle DCE $= 124°$. Find:
a) the area of the sector CDE
b) the area of triangle CDE
c) the area of the shaded segment.

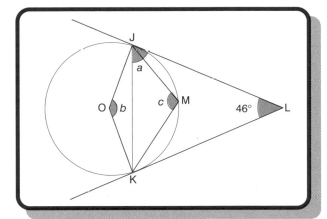

3 PR goes through O, the centre of the circle. Angle PRQ $= 55°$ and angle PQS $= 25°$. Find:
a) angle QSR **b)** angle POS **c)** angle OSR.

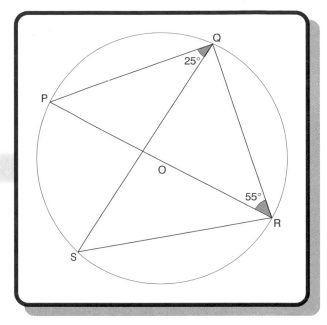

4 ABC is a sector of a circle centred at A, and with radius 18.4 mm. Find:
a) the length of the minor arc BC
b) the area of the sector.

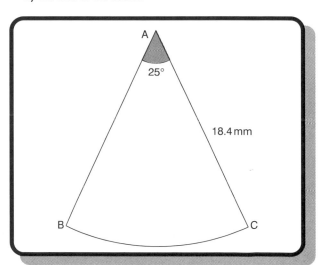

5 AB is a tangent to a circle with centre O, and C, D, E, F and G are points on the circumference such that angle OCF = 28°. Find angles x and y, giving reasons for your answers.

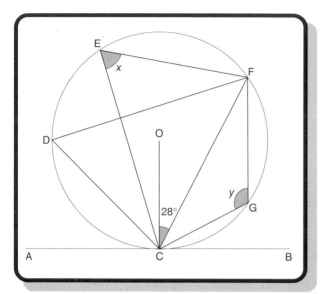

6 ABCE is a rectangle. AB = 5 cm and AE = 6 cm. CED is a quadrant of a circle centred at E. Find:
a) the perimeter of the shape   **b)** the area.

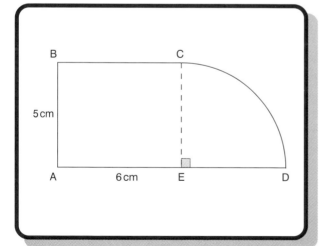

7 HJKL is a rectangle and HJ is a chord of a circle centred at M.
a) Using the cosine rule, find the angle HMJ.
b) Find the area of the sector HMJ.
c) Find the area of triangle HMJ.
d) Hence or otherwise, find the area of the whole shape.

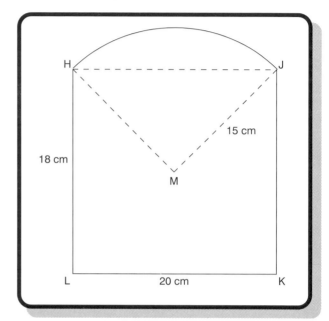

8 DEF is a sector of a circle centred at D. If the length of the minor arc EF is 4 cm, find θ to the nearest degree.

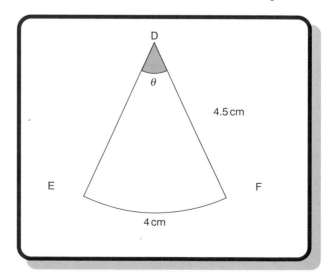

review

How much have you learnt?

Tick off each topic in the list when you are confident you can cope with it.

- ◯ Recognise cyclic quadrilaterals.
- ◯ Use the rules applying to cyclic quadrilaterals.
- ◯ Recognise angles, chords and tangents in circles.
- ◯ Use the basic rules that apply to angles, chords and tangents in circles.
- ◯ Find the area of a sector of a circle.
- ◯ Find the length of an arc of a circle.
- ◯ Find the area of a segment of a circle.

Answers

1 a) $67°$
  b) $134°$, OJL is a right-angled triangle.
  c) $113°$ ($\frac{1}{2}$ of the reflex angle at O)
2 a) $60.9\,cm^2$ b) $23.3\,cm^2$ c) $37.6\,cm^2$.
3 a) $35°$ (angle PQR = $90°$)
  b) $50°$ (Angle at centre of circle is twice the angle at the circumference.)
  c) $25°$ (Triangle ORS is isosceles.)
4 a) $8.0\,mm$ b) $73.9\,mm^2$
5 a) $x = 62°$ (alternate segment theorem, angle FCB = angle CEF)
  b) $y = 118°$ (opposite angles of a cyclic quadrilateral)
6 a) $29.9\,cm$ b) $49.6\,cm^2$
7 a) $83.6°$ b) $164.2\,cm^2$ c) $111.8\,cm^2$ d) $412.4\,cm^2$
8 $51°$

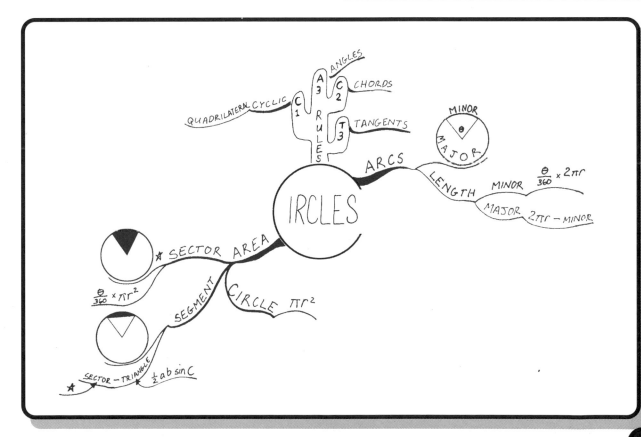

Transformations

9

REWARD

FOR INFORMATION LEADING TO THE ARREST OF TRANSFORMATIONS...

DEAD OR ALIVE

Reflection	1	• equation of the line
Rotation	3	• centre
		• direction (except if it is 180°)
		• size of angle
Enlargement	2	• centre
		• scale factor
Translation	1	• vector

preview

By the end of this chapter you will be able to:

- **recognise the transformations: reflection, rotation, enlargement and translation**

- **find the scale factor of an enlargement**

- **recognise vector quantities**

- **combine two vectors by drawing triangles and using trigonometry**

- **solve problems involving practical applications of vectors**

Transformations in the plane

The numbers next to each type of transformation show how many extra points you can pick up by including all the relevant pieces of information.

To find the scale factor of an enlargement

Second Over FirsT (SOFT)

You need the ratio of the image length to the original length.

$$\text{scale factor} = \frac{\text{image length}}{\text{original length}}$$

Compare this with scale factors in Chapter 7, Length, area and volume.

If the scale factor is less than 1, the 'enlargement' will in fact be smaller than the original.

Could you ride these horses in the rodeo?

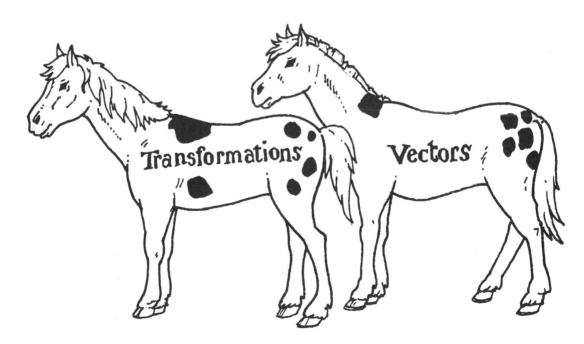

Vectors

Vectors represent movement. Vectors are written in columns, with the horizontal component (the movement in the x-direction) above the vertical component (the movement in the y-direction).

Always follow the direction of the arrow.

Remember that you can also go in the negative direction.

Vector notation can be confusing!

- **OA** may also be written as **a** or $\overrightarrow{OA}$
- **AO** is the same as –**a** or $\overrightarrow{AO}$
- **AB** = **AO** + **OB** = –**OA** + **OB** = –**a** + **b** = **b** – **a**

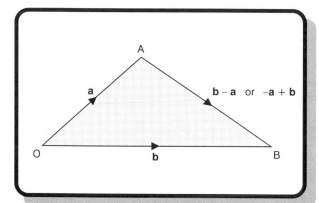

Example 9.1

In the diagram below, **OB** = **x**, **OD** = **y** and **OA** = **DC**.

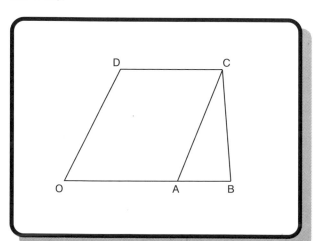

a) If **DC** = $\frac{2}{3}$**OB**, find **DC** in terms of **x** and **y**.

b) Find **CA**.

c) Is OACD a parallelogram? Justify your answer.

d) Give **CB** in terms of **x** and **y**.

Solution

a) **DC** = $\frac{2}{3}$**x** or $\frac{2\mathbf{x}}{3}$

b) **CA** = **CD** + **DO** + **OA** = $-\frac{2}{3}$**x** – **y** + $\frac{2}{3}$**x** = –**y**

c) OACD is a parallelogram because both pairs of opposite sides are parallel and equal in length.

d) **CB** = **CD** + **DO** + **OB** = $-\frac{2}{3}$**x** – **y** + **x** = $\frac{1}{3}$**x** – **y**

A vector has **magnitude** (i.e. size) and **direction**.

The magnitude of a vector is represented by its length. You can find this by using Pythagoras' theorem.

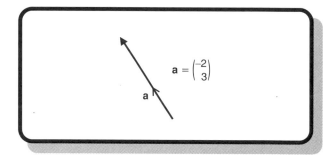

For example, the magnitude of $\begin{pmatrix} -2 \\ 3 \end{pmatrix}$ is $\sqrt{2^2 + 3^2}$ = 3.6.

The direction of a vector is the angle that the vector makes with a given direction.

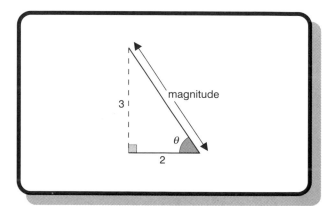

For example, the direction of $\begin{pmatrix} -2 \\ 3 \end{pmatrix}$ is

$\theta = \tan^{-1}(3 \div 2) = 56.3°$ to the negative x-direction.

The difference between velocity and speed

Velocity has magnitude and direction and can be represented by a vector, but speed is just the magnitude of that vector.

Vectors applied to boats in the moving water and planes in the air

In these questions, you have to construct a right-angled triangle. You need to consider:

- the direction the person would be going if there were no current or wind

- the air or water current

- the resultant direction (the direction in which the person is actually going).

Draw all the velocities on one right-angled triangle, and all the distances on another.

When drawing the velocities, start by drawing a line for the direction that the person would be moving if the water were still. At the end of this line, draw the direction of the current. Join the free ends of these two lines to make a right-angled triangle. The third length is the resultant velocity. It usually helps to make the velocity triangle smaller than the distance triangle. These two triangles will be similar.

Most questions can be solved using X-Direct, trigonometry, Pythagoras' theorem or the STV triplet.

Example 9.2

It's getting late and Chief Wairameye has found himself on the wrong side of the Mississuppa River. He can paddle his canoe at 0.6 m/s in still water. The river runs at right angles to the bank at a speed of 0.35 m/s. He needs to cross from point A to B, the nearest point on the opposite bank.

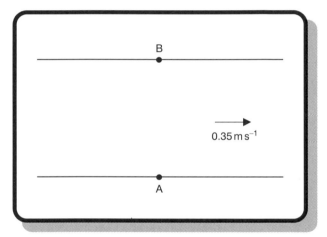

a) Find, by calculation, the direction to AB in which he must head initially.

b) Calculate his resultant speed in the direction AB.

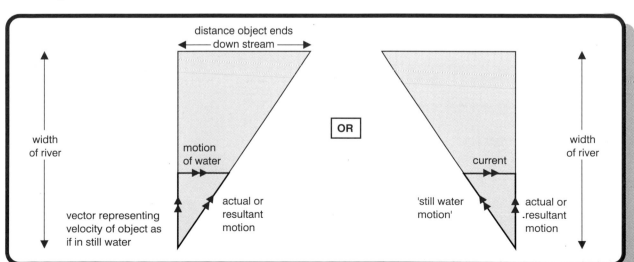

c) If the river is 200 m wide, how long does it take him to cross? Give your answer to the nearest 10 seconds.

d) If he aims the boat continually in a direction perpendicular to the flow of the water, how far downstream from B will he land?

Solution

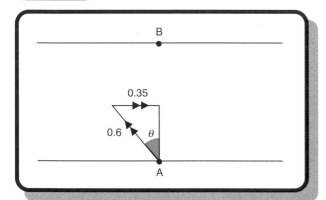

a) $\sin^{-1}(0.35 \div 0.6) = 35.7°$

b) $\sqrt{0.6^2 - 0.35^2} = 0.49\,\text{m/s}$

c) Using the STV triplet:

$$\text{time} = \frac{200}{0.49} = 410 \text{ seconds}$$

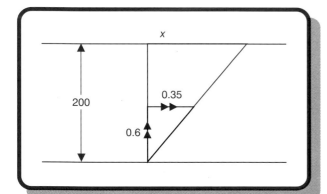

d) Speed　　　　Distance

　　0.6 　　　　　　200

　　0.35

$$\text{Distance} = \frac{0.35 \times 200}{0.6} = 117\,\text{m}$$

Exercise 9.1

1

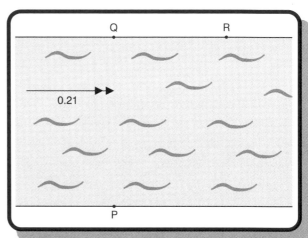

The diagram above illustrates a river flowing at 0.21 m/s and shows points P, Q and R where P is directly opposite Q. Chief Wairameye has got lost again. He finds himself stranded at P. The only two landing points on the other side of the river are at Q and R. The river is 60 m wide and Q is 45 m from R.

a) If Chief Wairameye swims at 0.3 m/s in still water, at what angle to PR must he head in order to land at Q?

b) If he now swims in a direction perpendicular to the bank, how fast must he swim to land at R?

c) What is his resultant speed in the direction PR?

2

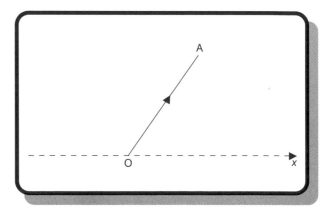

If the vector **OA** = $\begin{pmatrix} 5 \\ 12 \end{pmatrix}$, find:

a) its magnitude

b) the angle it makes with the x-axis.

3 In the triangle OAB, P is the midpoint of OA, and Q is the midpoint of OB.

If **OA** = **a** and **OB** = **b**, express, in terms of **a** and **b**:
a) AB   **b)** PQ   **c)** AQ.
d) Are AB and PQ parallel? Give reasons for your answer.

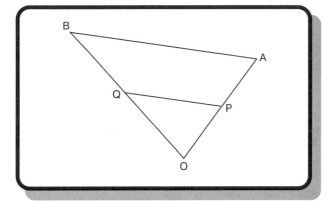

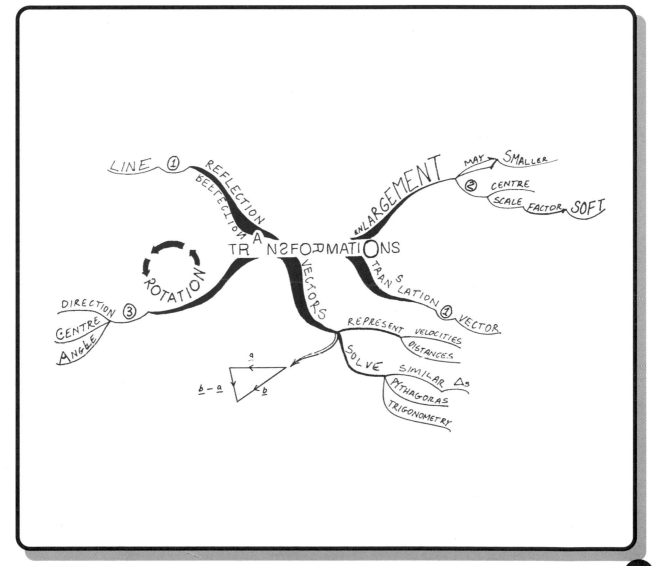

TAKE A BREAK

*Take a break and translate all this
information onto your mind map.*

Sharpen your spurs!

Exam-type questions 9

1 In the diagram below, what transformation maps:
   a) P on to Q
   b) Q on to R?
   c) What single transformation maps P on to R?

2 In the regular hexagon below, **OP** = **p** and **OQ** = **q**.
   Express the following in terms of **p** and **q**.
   a) QR   **b) OR**   **c) UQ**

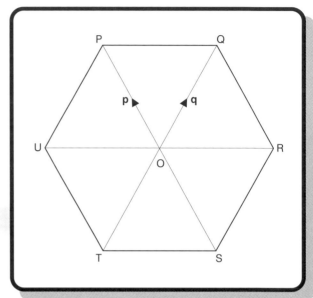

3 A woman can swim at 0.3 m/s in
   still water. The current in a river
   40 m wide flows at a speed of
   0.55 m/s in a direction parallel with
   the banks. If she always faces in a
   direction perpendicular to the flow
   of the current, find:
   a) her resultant speed,
   b) the direction from the bank in
   which she travels
   c) how far downstream she lands.

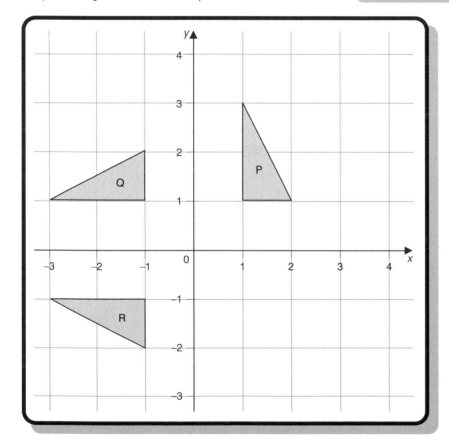

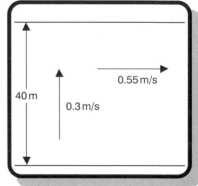

4 From the diagram below, what single transformation maps triangle T on to:
a) P   **b)** Q   **c)** R?

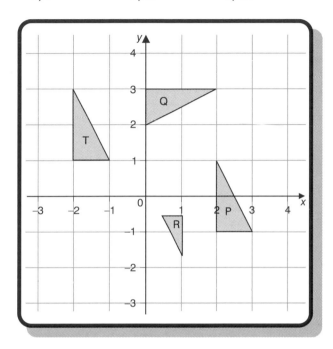

review

How much have you learnt?

Tick off each topic in the list when you are confident you can cope with it.

- Recognise the transformations: reflection, rotation, enlargement and translation.

- Find the scale factor of an enlargement.

- Recognise vector quantities.

- Combine two vectors by drawing triangles and using trigonometry.

- Solve problems involving practical applications of vectors.

5 An aeroplane can fly at 190 km/h in still air.
   a) If the wind blows in an easterly direction, with speed 80 km/h, on what bearing must the plane head in order to travel due north?
   b) What will its resultant speed be?

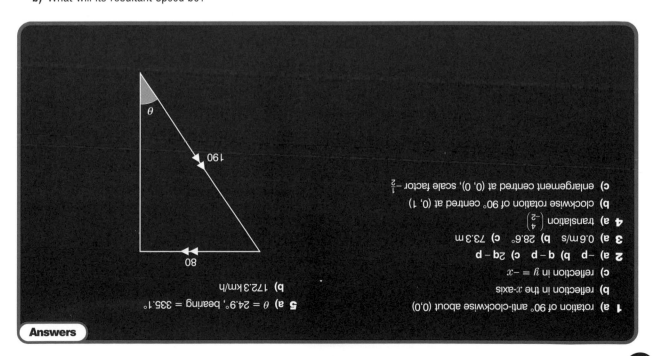

Answers

5 a) $\theta = 24.9°$, bearing = 335.1°   **b)** 172.3 km/h

1 a) rotation of 90° anti-clockwise about (0,0)
   b) reflection in the x-axis
   c) reflection in $y = -x$
2 a) $-\mathbf{p}$ **b)** $\mathbf{q} - \mathbf{p}$ **c)** $2\mathbf{q} - \mathbf{p}$
3 a) 0.6 m/s   **b)** 28.6°   **c)** 73.3 m
4 a) translation $\begin{pmatrix} 4 \\ -2 \end{pmatrix}$
   b) clockwise rotation of 90° centred at (0, 1)
   c) enlargement centred at (0, 0), scale factor $-\frac{1}{2}$

10

Do you bottle out on any of these?

Averages · Measures of spread · Bar charts and Histograms · Pie charts · Cumulative frequency · Scatter diagrams · Surveys and sampling

preview

- **calculate or evaluate the mean, median and mode of a set of data**

- **find the range of a set of data**

- **find the quartiles and percentiles of a range of data**

- **find the mean from a grouped frequency**

- **draw bar charts and histograms**

- **find and interpret frequency density**

- **draw and interpret pie charts**

- **draw a frequency polygon**

- **complete a cumulative frequency chart**

- **calculate the cumulative frequency for a set of data**

- **find the median from a cumulative frequency**

- **identify and use the interquartile range**

- **draw and interpret scatter diagrams**

- **evaluate sampling methods**

- **define data as discrete, continuous, quantitative or qualitative**

- **evaluate methods of collecting data**

Averages

The mean, the median and the mode are three ways of expressing the average.

This chart summarises how to find the mean, median and mode.

mean	Add together all the values and divide by the number of values you have. (The mean is not necessarily a whole number.)
median	Arrange the values in order from smallest to largest. The median is the middle value (referred to as the $\frac{1}{2}(n + 1)$ value).
mode	This is the most commonly occurring value. (There can be more than one mode.)

Measures of spread

Range – the difference in value between the largest and smallest values.

Interquartile range – see cumulative frequency.

Standard deviation – the formula is given on the *Information and formulae sheet*, which you will be given for each exam, but using a calculator is much faster!

Find out how to use your calculator. They are all different, and the methods vary a lot from calculator to calculator.

Some exam questions require you to find standard deviation using a calculator method. This often involves changing your calculator to a statistics setting. Remember to change it back when you've finished.

The pros and cons of using the mean, median and mode

	Advantages	Disadvantages
mean	• most commonly used • easy to calculate	• can be misleading, as if one term is much bigger or much smaller than the others it distorts the mean
median	• often gives a truer picture of the situation • not so affected by extreme values as the mean	• not used very often in the real world • takes longer to calculate because values must first be arranged
mode	• unaffected by extreme values • very appropriate when you need to find the most common result (e.g. if you were a buyer for shoes you would want to know the most commonly bought sizes.)	• there may be more than one mode • it ignores much of the information

Grouped frequency

When you have a large number of values, the data are often given in grouped form.

Here is an example of grouped data. It shows the number of farmsteads near Bodge City.

Distance (d) in km from Bodge City	Frequency
1 km or less	10
$1 < d \leqslant 2$	15
$2 < d \leqslant 3$	5

$1 < d \leqslant 2$ means a distance between 1 and 2 kilometres, but not including exactly 1 km. A distance of 1 km or less could be written as $0 < d \leqslant 1$ or just $d \leqslant 1$.

Finding the mean from a grouped frequency

In a grouped frequency, you cannot be sure of any exact value, so always use the midpoint of any group.

Example 10.1

500 citizens of Bodge City were asked how far they lived from their town centre. Their answers were put in this table. Find the mean distance that a citizen lives from the centre of Bodge City.

Distance (d) between home and town centre (km)	Midpoint (km)	Frequency
1 km or less	0.5	142
$1 < d \leqslant 2$	1.5	108
$2 < d \leqslant 3$	2.5	250

Solution

To find the mean:

- multiply the frequency by the midpoint

- add the results

- divide this total by the total frequency in the usual way.

The mean is
$(0.5 \times 142 + 1.5 \times 108 + 2.5 \times 250) \div 500 = 1.72\,\text{km}$

Check, using your calculator.

Make sure that your answer is sensible. If it is obviously wrong, check that you have divided by the total frequency.

Frequency diagrams

Bar charts and histograms

With bar charts, the sample is split up into groups and the height of each bar shows the number of values in the group represented by that bar.

For histograms, the frequency is shown by the area of each bar, not by the height.

The frequency density shows the number of units vertically for every unit horizontally.

For example, Old Mary's Dairy puts 12 cows in each of three different fields of the same area but different dimensions.

If the fields are 2, 6 and 3 furrows wide, the frequency density shows the average number of cows in each furrow.

Old Mary employs Faithful Frank to feed her cows. Remembering Frank FeeDs CoWs gives the triplet relating frequency (F), frequency density (FD) and class width (CW).

$$F = FD \times CW$$

$$FD = \frac{F}{CW} \qquad CW = \frac{F}{FD}$$

Example 10.2

The Tumbleweed Boarding House in Arid Creek has 105 rooms for guests. The numbers of rooms in the different price ranges are as follows.

Cost (x) per room ($)	Frequency	Class width	Frequency density
$0 < x \leqslant 10$	10		
$10 < x \leqslant 25$	30		
$25 < x \leqslant 40$	45		
$40 < x \leqslant 45$	10		

a) Complete the table above.

b) Draw a histogram to represent the data.

c) What does the frequency density represent?

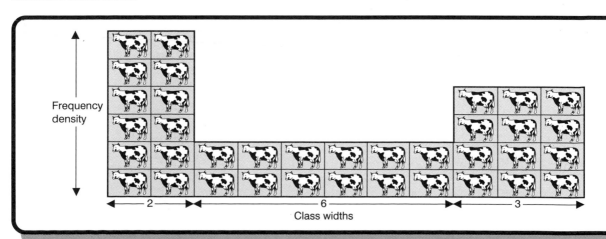

Frequency density

2   6   3

Class widths

Solution

a)

Cost (x) per room ($)	Frequency	Class width	Frequency density
$0 < x \leqslant 10$	10	10	1
$10 < x \leqslant 25$	30	15	2
$25 < x \leqslant 40$	45	15	3
$40 < x \leqslant 45$	10	5	2

b)

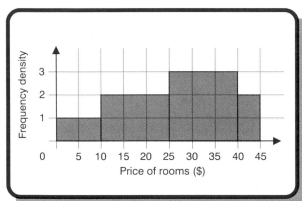

c) The frequency density is the number of rooms per $1 interval.

Exercise 10.1

To celebrate Chief Hiapottenyooz's birthday, the Kejeree tribe gets together for a party. The tribe is grouped according to age.

Age in years (x)	Frequency	Frequency density
$0 < x \leqslant 10$	100	
$10 < x \leqslant 20$	80	
$20 < x \leqslant 40$	100	
$40 < x \leqslant 55$	15	

1 Complete the table.

2 Complete the histogram.

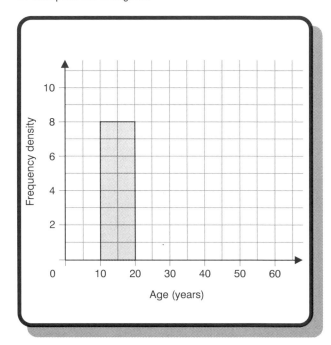

3 What does 1 square unit on the graph represent?

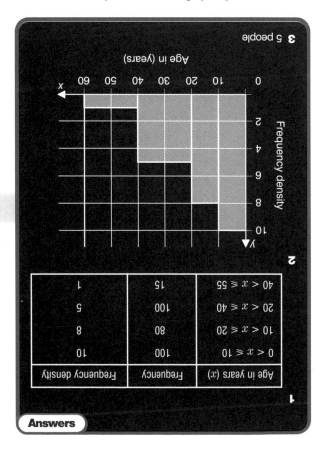

Answers

3 5 people

2

1

Age in years (x)	Frequency	Frequency density
$0 < x \leqslant 10$	100	10
$10 < x \leqslant 20$	80	8
$20 < x \leqslant 40$	100	5
$40 < x \leqslant 55$	15	1

Pie charts

Pie charts are another way of showing frequency. The whole circle (360°) represents the entire sample. Each sector of the pie chart relates to a grouping from the sample.

It may help to use X-Direct.

Example 10.3

A pie chart is used to represent the mix of peoples in the State of Aridzona. A sector of angle 70° represents the 448 members of the Komansee tribe.

a) What is the size of the Chinnup tribe, whose sector has an angle of 80°?

b) What is the total population of the State?

Solution

a)

	Degrees	People
Komansee	70	448
Chinnup	80	

Size of Chinnup Tribe $= \dfrac{80 \times 448}{70} = 512$

b)

	Degrees	People
	70	448
	360	

Number of people in the State

$= \dfrac{360 \times 448}{70} = 2304$

Frequency polygons

These are closely related to bar charts. A frequency polygon is a line on a graph connecting the midpoints of the tops of the bars, in order (but the bars themselves are not drawn on a frequency polygon).

Cumulative frequency

To find the cumulative frequency you accumulate (i.e. build up) a running total of the frequencies, starting from the first, until you have included the values of the whole group.

Always write the cumulative frequency on the vertical axis.

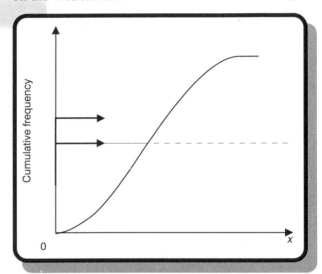

To find the median from a cumulative frequency

As samples usually involve large numbers, we can simply divide the total frequency by 2 to find the position of the median without unduly distorting the result.

Lower and upper quartiles

As the word 'quartile' might suggest, these split the sample into quarters. The lower quartile is the item of data 'a quarter of the way up'. The median is the item of data 'halfway up'. The upper quartile is the item 'three-quarters of the way up'. To find the value of:

a) the lower quartile (LQ), divide the total frequency by 4

b) the upper quartile (UQ), multiply the number you found for the LQ by 3 (i.e. it is three-quarters of the sample).

10

Percentiles

Percentiles divide the data into hundredths. The median is at the 50th percentile, the lower quartile is at the 25th percentile, and the upper quartile is at the 75th percentile. To find any percentile, take this percentage of the total sample, and continue as for the median.

Interquartile range

Interquartile range
= upper quartile – lower quartile

What does the interquartile range tell you?

The interquartile range shows you how widely the central half of the sample is spread. A low interquartile range shows that the data are closely grouped together, whereas a higher figure would reflect wider differences between the data (also called a wider spread). This is closely related to the standard deviation.

Example 10.4

The Komansee and Chinnup tribes have an annual markspersonship contest! Their results for this year are as follows.

Interquartile range	Komansee	10
Interquartile range	Chinnup	25

What do these figures tell us?

Solution

The interquartile range of the Komansees' results is smaller than that of the Chinnups. This shows that their markspersonship is more consistent than that of the Chinnups.

Note that the interquartile range does not tell you which class had the better performance – one of the measures of the average would tell you this.

Scatter diagrams

Two sets of data can be plotted on a set of axes. The scatter diagram shows how the data relate to each other. The **line of best fit** is a line that passes through – or close to – most of the points.

Correlation shows a link between the variables on both axes.

Positive correlation – if one variable rises the other is expected to rise.

Strong positive correlation

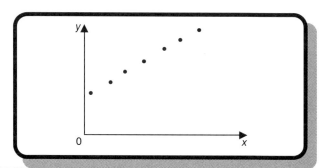

Moderate positive correlation

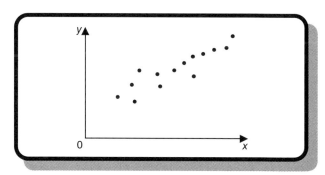

Negative correlation – if one variable goes up, the other will probably fall.

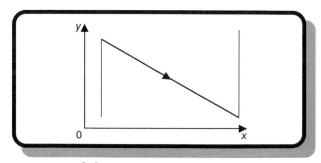

Remember **N** for negative correlation.

Strong negative correlation

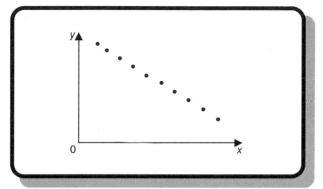

Moderate negative correlation

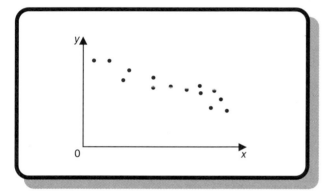

No correlation – there is no link between the two variables.

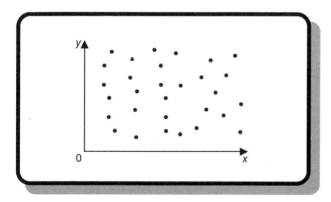

TAKE A BREAK

This is another good place to take a break before you take a run at the rest of this chapter.

Sampling

In any statistical research, it is impossible to collect data from every possible unit which may be involved. It is necessary, therefore, to take a sample which is a good cross-section of the whole.

You are often asked to comment on a sample. There are three main points to consider.

- Size – is the sample big enough?
- Representativeness – are all types represented?
- Randomness – is the sample biased in any way?

Remember these – if not, you'll be SoRRy.

Sampling methods

Random sampling – everybody has an equal chance of being chosen.

Stratified or stratified random sampling – a sample is selected according to certain criteria, but within that group the sample is random.

Data definitions

Discrete – every value is separate from the next value e.g. number of cars

Continuous – every value is on a sliding scale e.g. temperature

Qualitative – information on people's opinions

Quantitative – numerical data

Surveys

Examiners sometimes ask you to give your opinion on surveys and questionnaires. You should comment upon each of the following.

1 *The way the question is worded*
   a) leading (i.e. trying to push the interviewee into answering in a certain way)
   b) ambiguous (i.e. the question could be interpreted in more than one way)

2 *The range of responses*
   This is less common, but you should look at ways which the interviewee can reply to see whether all possible outcomes are clearly and accurately represented.

3 *Drawing up questionnaires*
   Use the above criteria and avoid the pitfalls.

   Is the question:
   Ambiguous? **L**eading? **I**nclusive? **BI**ased?

   Remember, you always need an ALIBI!

No pain, no gain!

Exam-type questions 10

1 The Chief's son, Eyecountum, drew a pie chart to show how many braves had paid their Arrow Tax. If θ is the angle representing 20 people, express, in terms of θ:
   a) the angle representing 30 people
   b) the angle representing the other people not already mentioned in the sample.

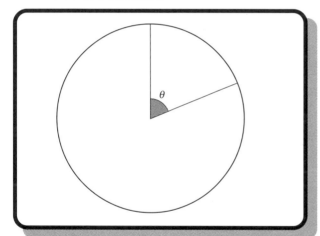

2 The table below gives the exam marks out of 40 gained by 80 pupils.

Marks (x)	Frequency	Cumulative frequency
$0 < x \leqslant 5$	0	
$5 < x \leqslant 10$	2	
$10 < x \leqslant 15$	6	
$15 < x \leqslant 20$	18	
$20 < x \leqslant 25$	20	
$25 < x \leqslant 30$	16	
$30 < x \leqslant 35$	12	
$35 < x \leqslant 40$	6	

a) Complete the table and draw the cumulative frequency curve.
b) Find approximate answers for the upper quartile, lower quartile and interquartile range.
c) The top 35% pass the test. Find the 65th percentile and hence the pass mark.
d) The top five people win a prize. What is the minimum mark for a prize?

3 Draw a frequency polygon to illustrate the information in question **2**.
a) What is the modal class?
b) How can you tell this from the diagram?

4 Using the information in question **2**, find the mean.

5 The sketch below shows three normal distributions.

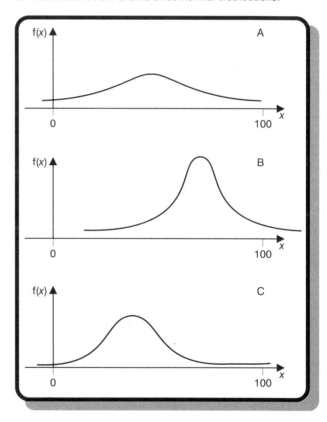

a) Which has the highest mean?
b) Which has the highest standard deviation?

6 The table below shows the time taken by contestants to complete a puzzle.

Time in minutes	0 – 5	5 – 10	10 – 20	20 – 35	35 – 40
No. of competitors	10	35	30	15	10

Complete the histogram using the above information.

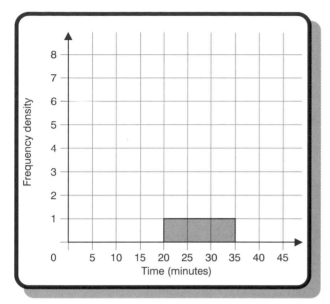

7 a) Draw the line of best fit on the diagram below.

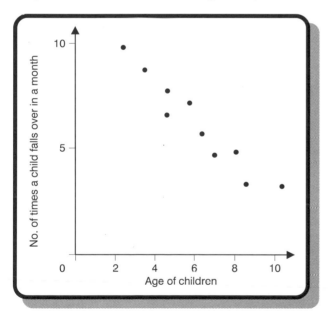

b) How would you describe the correlation in the scatter diagram?

c) Why is your line of best fit misleading when trying to predict results for babies under 2 or children over 10?

8 Do you read magazines about pop music?

Answer | Yes/No |

a) How would you improve this question?

b) Would you use a random or stratified sample when conducting a survey of this form? Justify your answer.

9 A sample was taken of the telephone calls made from a certain call box. The lengths of the calls, in minutes, are as shown on the graph below.

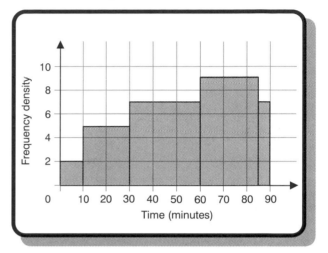

Complete the table.

Length of call (x)	Frequency
$0 < x \leqslant 10$	
$10 < x \leqslant 30$	100
$30 < x \leqslant 60$	
$60 < x \leqslant 85$	
$85 < x \leqslant 90$	

10 Using the formula, or otherwise, find the standard deviation for the following sample.

1, 1, 4, 5, 5, 7, 10, 11, 11

11 A survey was carried out on the life, in hours, of two brands of batteries A and B. The sample consisted of 40 batteries of each type. The cumulative frequency graph drawn below illustrates the performance of one brand.

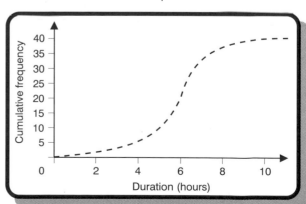

The results for the other brand are as follows.

Life in hours (x)	Frequency
$0 < x \leq 2$	4
$2 < x \leq 4$	7
$4 < x \leq 6$	9
$6 < x \leq 8$	14
$8 < x \leq 10$	6

a) On the graph given, draw the cumulative frequency graph using this data.
b) If B has the smaller interquartile range, label the graphs as A and B.
c) Which brand is better value? Give a reason for your choice.

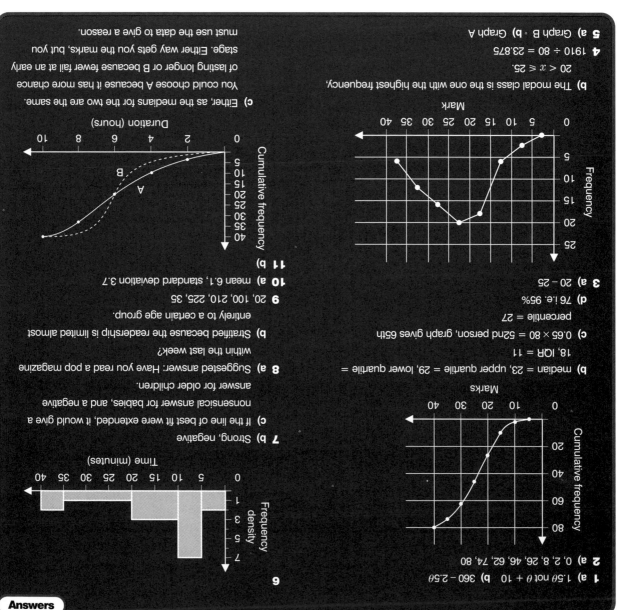

Answers

1 a) 1.5θ not $\theta + 10$ **b)** $360 - 2.5\theta$

2 a) 0, 2, 8, 26, 46, 62, 74, 80

3 a) $20 - 25$

b) median = 23, upper quartile = 29, lower quartile =
   18, IQR = 11

c) $0.65 \times 80 = 52$nd person, graph gives 65th
   percentile = 27

d) 76 i.e. 95%

4 $1910 \div 80 = 23.875$
   $20 < x \leq 25.$

b) The modal class is the one with the highest frequency.

5 a) Graph B **b)** Graph A

6

7 b) Strong, negative

c) If the line of best fit were extended, it would give a
   nonsensical answer for babies, and a negative
   answer for older children.

8 a) Suggested answer: Have you read a pop magazine
   within the last week?

b) Stratified because the readership is limited almost
   entirely to a certain age group.

9 20, 100, 210, 225, 35

10 a) mean 6.1, standard deviation 3.7

11 b)

c) Either, as the medians for the two are the same.
   You could choose A because it has more chance
   of lasting longer or B because fewer fail at an early
   stage. Either way gets you the marks, but you
   must use the data to give a reason.

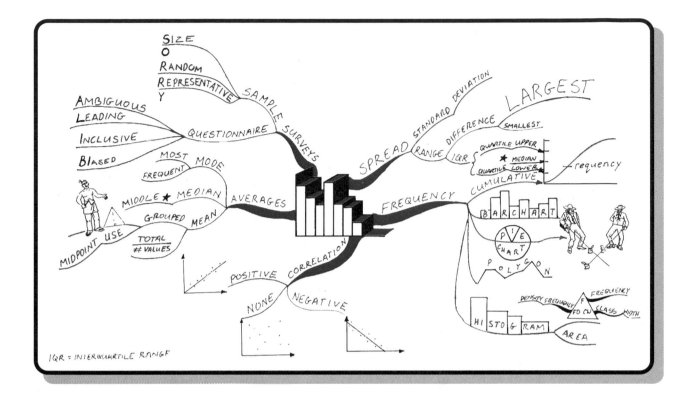

IQR = INTERQUARTILE RANGE

review

How much have you learnt?

Tick off each topic in the list when you are confident you can cope with it.

○ Calculate or evaluate the mean, median and mode of a set of data.

○ Find the range of a set of data.

○ Find the quartiles and percentiles of a range of data.

○ Complete a cumulative frequency chart.

○ Find the mean from a grouped frequency.

○ Draw bar charts and histograms.

○ Find and interpret frequency density.

○ Draw and interpret pie charts.

○ Draw a frequency polygon.

○ Calculate the cumulative frequency for a set of data.

○ Find the median from a cumulative frequency.

○ Identify and use the interquartile range.

○ Draw and interpret scatter diagrams.

○ Evaluate sampling methods.

○ Define data as discrete, continuous, quantitative or qualitative.

○ Evaluate methods of collecting data.

Probability

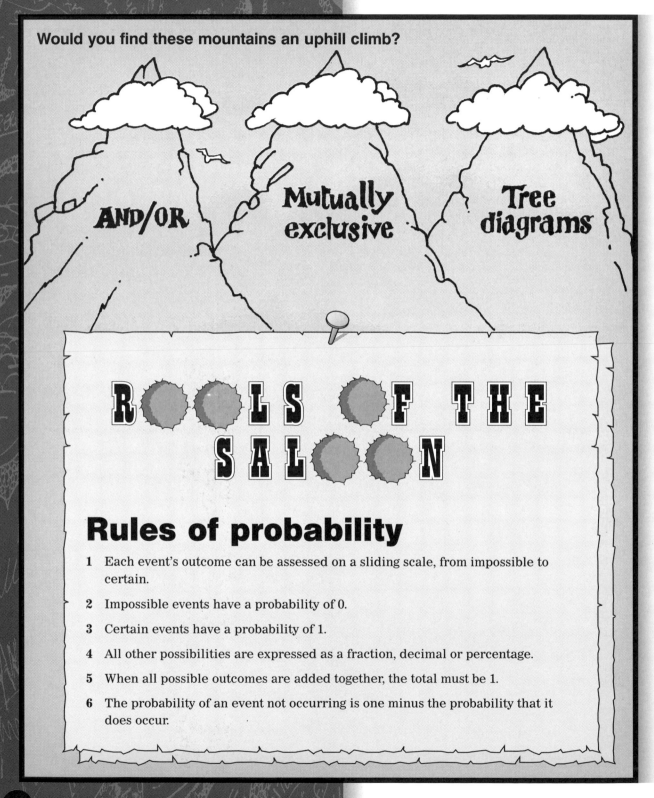

11

Would you find these mountains an uphill climb?

AND/OR

Mutually exclusive

Tree diagrams

ROOLS OF THE SALOON

Rules of probability

1　Each event's outcome can be assessed on a sliding scale, from impossible to certain.

2　Impossible events have a probability of 0.

3　Certain events have a probability of 1.

4　All other possibilities are expressed as a fraction, decimal or percentage.

5　When all possible outcomes are added together, the total must be 1.

6　The probability of an event not occurring is one minus the probability that it does occur.

preview

By the end of this chapter you will be able to:

- **use the rules of probability**

- **identify mutually exclusive events**

- **draw tree diagrams to evaluate probabilities**

- **calculate probabilities for events carried out 'without replacement'**

Calculating probability

$$\text{probability} = \frac{\text{number of required outcomes}}{\text{number of possible outcomes}}$$

Example 11.1

Double-Dealing Dennis gets people to pick out two cards from a full pack with replacement (i.e. once a card is picked, it is returned to the pack). What is the probability of picking two red cards?

The combinations are

1st card	2nd card
R	R
R	B
B	R
B	B

Solution

You could use AND.

The probability of drawing a red card first time $= \frac{1}{2}$.

If you want two reds, you want a red AND another red.

$\frac{1}{2} \times \frac{1}{2} = \frac{1}{4}$

In most questions of probability,

 ADORE MEANS ADD = OR

 SAND TIMER   TIMES = AND

 AND   OR

Mutually exclusive events

These are events that cannot occur at the same time. For example, night and day are mutually exclusive because they never occur at the same time.

If the events are mutually exclusive you can use ADORE (OR = ADD), but when they are not mutually exclusive you cannot.

Tree diagrams

Example 11.2

Bodge City's posse is recruiting new members. Recruits must undergo two tests. The probability of passing the first, a sharp-shooting test, is $\frac{3}{5}$, and the probability of passing the second, a bareback riding test, is $\frac{2}{3}$. Draw a tree diagram to illustrate this.

What is the probability that a candidate taken at random:

a) passes both parts

b) fails the first but passes the second

c) passes one test, but not both?

Solution

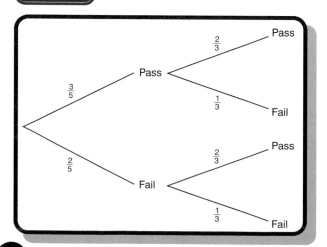

a) Reword the question as 'Find the probability of passing the first AND the second.'

$$\frac{3}{5} \times \frac{2}{3} = \frac{6}{15} = \frac{2}{5}$$

b) Reword the question as 'fails the first AND passes the second'.

$$\frac{2}{5} \times \frac{2}{3} = \frac{4}{15}$$

c) Reword as '(fails the first AND passes the second) OR (passes the first AND fails the second)'.

$$\frac{2}{5} \times \frac{2}{3} + \frac{3}{5} \times \frac{1}{3} = \frac{4}{15} + \frac{3}{15}$$
$$= \frac{7}{15}$$

Be careful when finding total probability. For example, when you roll two dice, you have 36 different outcomes – i.e. the product of 6 and 6 not the sum of 6 and 6.

Probability without replacement

Example 11.3

The Bodge City Posse owns three brown horses, two black horses and four grey horses. Two members rush out and grab the first two they can catch.

a) Using the above example, draw a tree diagram to illustrate all possible outcomes.

b) Find the probability they are both brown.

c) What is the probability that both horses are of the same colour?

d) What is the probability that both horses are of different colour?

Solution

a) Method for drawing the tree diagram:
   i) The first person has 9 horses to choose from, so the second person has 8. Fill in all the denominators first.
   ii) The numerators for the first horse chosen are simple – they are the numbers given.
   iii) Look at each second stage in turn – e.g. if a brown horse was chosen first, there are two brown left but the others remain unchanged.

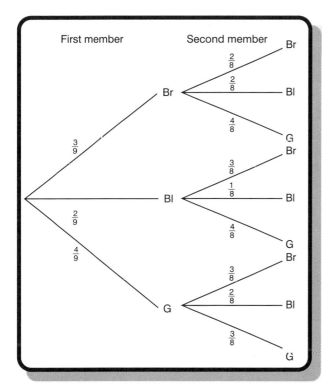

b) The question can be reworded as 'a brown first AND a brown second'.

The probability that the first horse is brown is $\frac{3}{9}$. (Do not cancel at this stage.)

You are now left with a total of eight horses, two of which are brown, so the probability that your second horse is brown is $\frac{2}{8}$.

So the probability that both are brown
$= \frac{3}{9} \times \frac{2}{8} = \frac{6}{72} = \frac{1}{12}$

(You should always cancel at the end where possible.)

c) If they are both the same colour, they could be:

brown and brown or black and black or grey and grey

$\frac{3}{9} \times \frac{2}{8} + \frac{2}{9} \times \frac{1}{8} + \frac{4}{9} \times \frac{3}{8} = \frac{5}{18}$

d) If the horses are not of different colours, they must be the same colour.

P(they are of different colours)
= 1 – P(they are the same colour)
= $\frac{13}{18}$

Exercise 11.1

1 Chief Wairameye is lost again. He is at point A and his tribe's settlement is at Z. At each junction A, P and Q he has an equal probability of turning right or left. What is the probability that he reaches home?

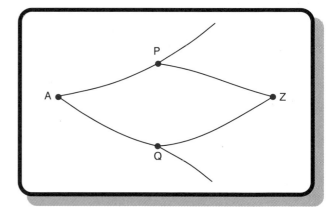

2 In Arid Creek there are three associations: the Ranchwomen's Guild, which only allows women as members, the Gentlemen-only Bareback Riders association, and the church which welcomes everybody. If the probabilities of a person picked at random joining one of these groups are 0.2, 0,15 and 0.45 respectively, would you expect the probability of a person belonging to:
a) the Ranchwomen or the church to be 0.65
b) the Ranchwomen or the Bareback Riders to be 0.35?
Give reasons for your answers.

3 Bodge City's General Store has Drooper's Brew and Trail Ale on special offer, but as usual the bottles are mixed up and unlabelled. At the end of the week, they have six bottles of Drooper's Brew and four of Trail Ale left. If two people buy one bottle each, find the probability that:
a) both bottles are Drooper's Brew
b) one bottle of each is sold.

The game's over!

Exam-type questions 11

1 Components in a machine have a 0.7 chance of being faulty. In a batch of 3000 machines, how many would you expect to find with a faulty component?

2 A sample is divided into the following groups.
a) men who wear glasses
b) men without glasses
c) women with glasses
d) women with hats

Which two groups are not mutually exclusive?

3 A game at a fair requires players to spin two unbiased spinners as shown below. The two numbers shown are then added.

a) List all possible outcomes.
b) What is the probability of scoring 5?
c) What is the probability of not scoring 7?
d) What is the probability of scoring more than 7?

4 The probability of passing a test first time was found to be 0.6. Students who retook the test had a failure rate of 0.3. Of those taking it a third time, 90% passed.
a) Draw a tree diagram below, showing this information.

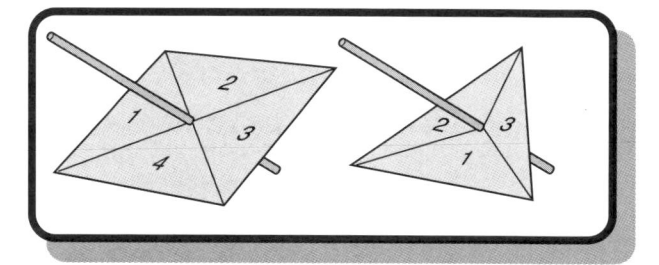

b) What is the probability of passing the test on the first or second attempt?
c) If 1000 people took the test, how many would you expect to fail at all three attempts?

Answers

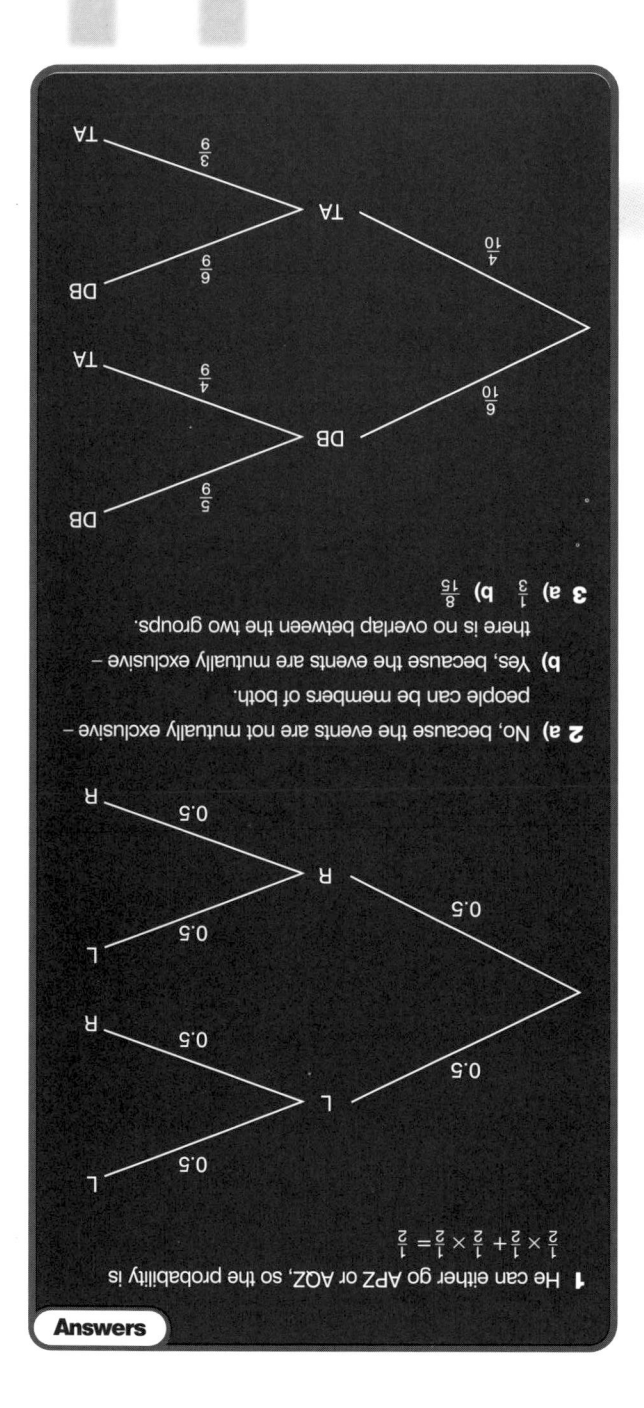

1 He can either go APZ or AQZ, so the probability is
$$\frac{1}{2} \times \frac{1}{2} + \frac{1}{2} \times \frac{1}{2} = \frac{1}{2}$$

2 a) No, because the events are not mutually exclusive – people can be members of both.
b) Yes, because the events are mutually exclusive – there is no overlap between the two groups.

3 a) $\frac{1}{3}$ **b)** $\frac{8}{15}$

TAKE A BREAK

Are you still with us? Take a break and congratulate yourself.

5 At a school fair, three competitors throw wet sponges at a teacher. If each has a 40% chance of hitting the target, find:
a) the probability that they all miss
b) the probability that only one will hit the teacher
c) the probability that the teacher will get wet.

6 Two people play a game which can either be won or lost. One player has a 0.25 chance of winning a game. If they play two games, find the probability that this player will:
a) win two games
b) win exactly one game.

review
How much have you learnt?

Tick off each topic in the list when you are confident you can cope with it.

- Use the rules of probability.
- Identify mutually exclusive events.
- Draw tree diagrams to evaluate probabilities.
- Calculate probabilities for events carried out 'without replacement'.

Answers

1 2100

2 c) and d)

3 a) 2, 3, 4, 5, 6, 7 are the possible outcomes
b) $\frac{3}{12} = \frac{1}{4}$ c) $\frac{11}{12}$ d) 0

4 a)

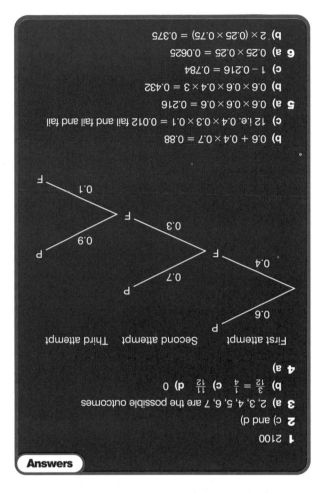

First attempt — Second attempt — Third attempt

b) $0.6 + 0.4 \times 0.7 = 0.88$
c) 12 i.e. $0.4 \times 0.3 \times 0.1 = 0.012$ fail and fail and fail

5 a) $0.6 \times 0.6 \times 0.6 = 0.216$
b) $0.6 \times 0.6 \times 0.4 \times 3 = 0.432$
c) $1 - 0.216 = 0.784$

6 a) $0.25 \times 0.25 = 0.0625$
b) $2 \times (0.25 \times 0.75) = 0.375$

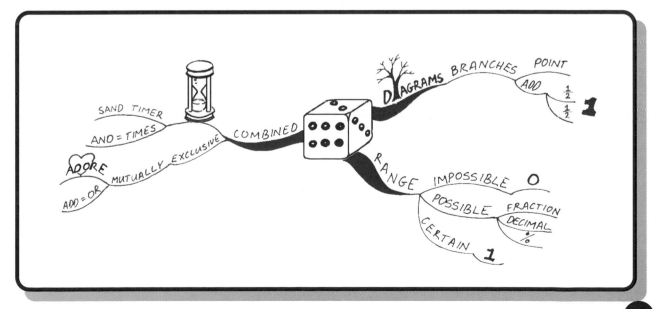

Countdown to the examination

TELLS YOU HOW

TOP SECRET

IMPORTANCE OF CHAPTERS

1 ONE
STATISTICS
GRAPHS
LENGTH, AREA +
VOLUME
PYTHAGORAS +
TRIGONOMETRY

2 TWO
ALGEBRA
PROBABILITY
NUMBER

3 THREE
PROPORTIONALITY
AND
PERCENTAGES
TRANSFORMATIONS

4 FOUR
CIRCLES
LOCI AND
CONSTRUCTIONS

Do you recognise yourself?

Read through the following categories to see which one best describes your current state of mind. Then look at Chief Icazaminna's advice for your type.

Type A

I'm in a panic.
I don't know where to start.
I'm running out of time.
I don't know how I'm going to remember everything.
My revision is up the spout.

Type B

I've worked hard, but my confidence could do with a boost.
I'm in with a chance, but I need more practice at examination type questions.
I'd like some help in organising my remaining revision time.

Type C

I've revised everything I can possibly think of.
I don't have (m)any problems with anything on the syllabus.
I'd enjoy tackling some more questions just for fun.

Chief Icazaminna says ...

Type A

Don't worry. You could still have time to put things right. Turn to page 140 and work through as much of Stages 1–3 as you can. If you can complete Stage 1, you have a good chance of passing, even though time is running out. If you manage to get through Stage 2, you may even scrape a B, and success with Stage 3 gives you a fighting chance of an A or A*, especially if you then work through the specimen examination papers.

Type B

Congratulations. You deserve to do well. Look at the opposite page and revise the chapters in the suggested order. Then try Specimen Examination Papers 1 and 2. Now make sure that you have covered everything by checking with Stages 1–3 on page 140. Then try the other two specimen examination papers.

Type C

You probably have your sights set on a high grade. Try the first two specimen examination papers and see how you get on. If you do well you should do the other two papers, just to make sure that there is nothing which could catch you out. After that, it's just a matter of turning up for the exams and then waiting to collect your A or A*.

All candidates – a last round up!

Chief Icazaminna invites you join him in Last Orders, page 145.

The party's really over now! It's time to get serious.

Paper 1

1 a) Evaluate $\dfrac{a(b + c)}{a^2 - c}$ when $a = 5.2$, $b = -0.1$, $c = 3.7$.

b) Rearrange the formula $R = 3(p - q^2)$ to make q the subject.

2 Express $2^3 \div 2^5$
a) as a power of 2   **b)** as a fraction.

3 Two fair six-sided dice are thrown. Find the probability of:
a) the sum of the two numbers on the dice being 10 or more
b) both dice showing the same number
c) both dice showing different numbers.

4 The lengths of telephone calls made by a household over the last 12 months were as follows.

Length of call (t minutes)	Frequency
$0 < t \le 5$	40
$5 < t \le 10$	30
$10 < t \le 20$	70
$20 < t \le 40$	60
$40 < t \le 80$	80

a) Complete the histogram on the diagram below.

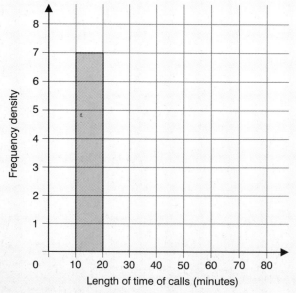

b) What does 1 square unit on the grid represent?

5 In the diagram below find:
a) BC   **b)** angle CDA.

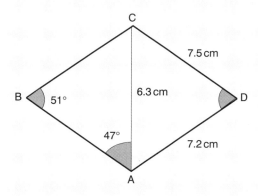

c) Using the area of a triangle $= \frac{1}{2}ab\sin C$, find the area of the entire shape.

6 a) Solve by factorisation $2x^2 + 9x - 5 = 0$.
b) Solve $3x^2 + 8x = 5$, giving your answers correct to 2 d.p.
c) Give the range of values for which $x^2 \le 4$.
d) Give the range of values for which $x^2 \ge 1$.

7 Two cylinders are similar. The larger holds 152 cm³ and the smaller holds 42 cm³. If the height of the larger is 25 cm, find the height of the smaller.

8 Write as an interval approximation 4.32 corrected to 2 d.p.

9 Write an expression for the nth term of each of the following sequences.

a) $\frac{1}{7}$, $\frac{2}{11}$, $\frac{3}{15}$, $\frac{4}{19}$ ...
b) $\frac{7}{9}$, $\frac{11}{12}$, $\frac{15}{17}$, $\frac{19}{24}$ ...

10 On the diagram below, sketch the graph of $y = \cos x$.

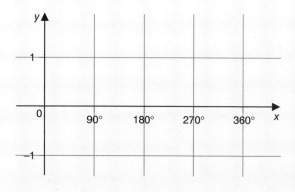

Hence or otherwise find two values of x, in the range $0° \le x < 360°$, such that $\cos x = -0.5$.

11 The diagram below shows the graph of $y = x^2 - 3x$.

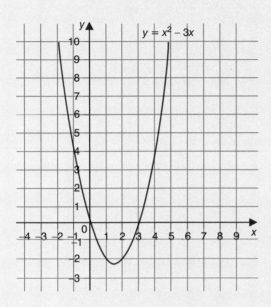

Using the graph, estimate the solutions of:
a) $x^2 - 3x = 5$ **b)** $x^2 - 4x - 2 = 0$.

12 Find the mean and standard deviation of:
3, 3, 7, 12, 13, 15, 15, 17, 18

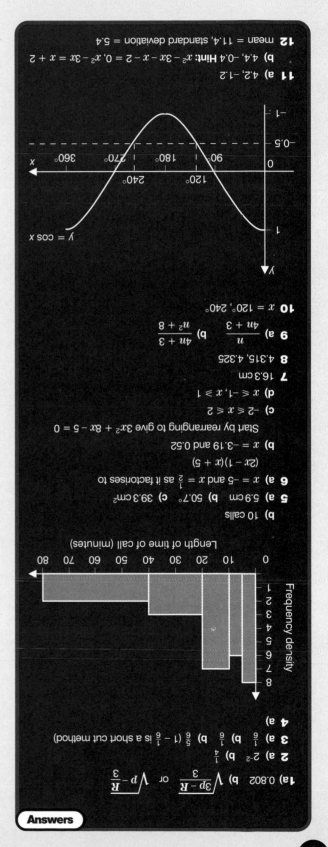

The answer panel (shown upside-down in the image) reads:

12 mean = 11.4, standard deviation = 5.4

11 a) 4.2, –1.2
b) 4.4, –0.4 **Hint:** $x^2 - 3x - x - 2 = 0$, $x^2 - 3x = x + 2$

$y = \cos x$

10 $x = 120°, 240°$

9 a) $\dfrac{n}{4n + 3}$ **b)** $\dfrac{n^2 + 8}{4n + 3}$

8 4.315, 4.325

7 16.3 cm

d) $x \geqslant -1, x \geqslant 1$
c) $-2 \leqslant x \leqslant 2$
Start by rearranging to give $3x^2 + 8x - 5 = 0$
b) $x = -3.19$ and 0.52
$(2x - 1)(x + 5)$
6 a) $x = -5$ and $x = \frac{1}{2}$ as it factorises to

5 a) 5.9 cm   **b)** 50.7°   **c)** 39.3 cm²
b) 10 calls

Length of time of call (minutes)

Frequency density

4 a)
3 a) $\frac{1}{6}$ **b)** $\frac{5}{6}$ $(1 - \frac{1}{6}$ is a short cut method)
2 a) 2·2   **b)** $\frac{1}{4}$
1a) 0.802   **b)** $\sqrt{\dfrac{3p - R}{3}}$ or $\sqrt{p - \dfrac{R}{3}}$

Answers

Paper 2

1 a) p is an integer other than 3 such that $\sqrt{p} \times \sqrt{3}$ is a rational number. Give a possible value for p.

b) Express 0.181 818... in the form $\frac{a}{b}$ where and a and b are integers.

c) Which of the following numbers are rational?

 i) 0.311 111 1... **ii)** $\frac{1}{\pi}$ **iii)** $\sqrt{2} \times 2\sqrt{2}$

2 The speed of light is approximately 3×10^8 m/s. Find the time light takes to travel 6.3×10^6 km.

3 In a bag of 17 marbles, 8 are blue and the rest are green. Two marbles are drawn from the bag without replacement.

a) Draw a tree diagram to illustrate this information.

b) What is the probability of the marbles being of different colours?

c) What is the probability that the marbles are of the same colour?

4 In the diagram below, find:

a) the length OQ correct to one decimal place

b) angle QOR to the nearest degree.

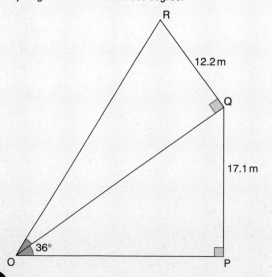

5 These are marks given in a test for a group of students.

Marks	Number of students
0 – 20	4
21 – 40	44
41 – 60	100
61 – 80	30
81 – 100	22

a) Illustrate this on the cumulative frequency diagram below.

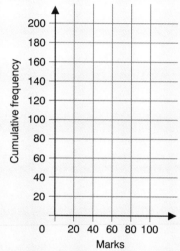

b) From your diagram, find the median and the interquartile range.

c) A student was told that she was at the 80th percentile. What mark did she obtain?

d) What percentage of students scored above 70 marks?

6 A river is 50 m wide. The current is flowing at 0.15 m/s in a direction parallel to the bank. A woman at P can swim at 0.4 m/s in still water. She is continually aiming in a direction perpendicular to the bank.

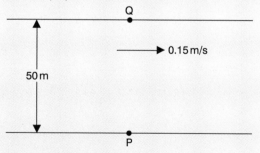

a) How far downstream will she land?

b) Find her resultant speed.

7 a) Solve the following equations.

$2x - 5y = 20$

$3x - 4y = 23$

b) Find x where $7 - 8x = x + 2$, expressing your answer as a fraction.

8 If the height of a piece of paper was given as 11 cm and the area as 88 cm² (both measurements given correct to the nearest whole number), find:

a) the maximum width **b)** the minimum width.

9 ABCD is a cyclic quadrilateral in the circle centre O. XY is a tangent to the circle at C. Angle BCY = 37°. Angle DBC = 42°. Find:

a) angle CDB **b)** angle DAB.

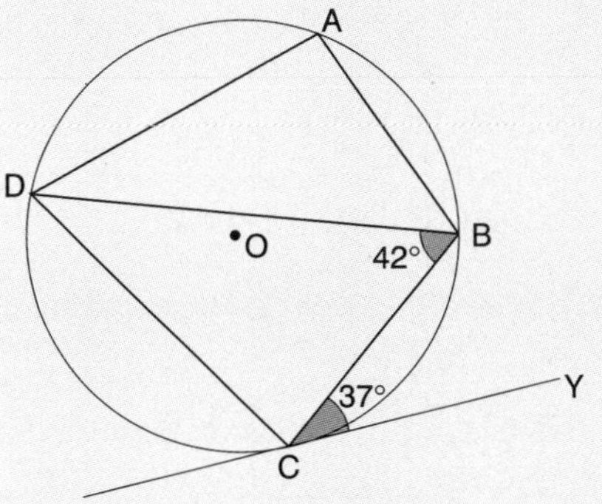

10 On the diagram below, indicate the required region such that:

$4x + 3y \leqslant 24 \quad 2x + 3y \leqslant 18 \quad x \geqslant 2 \quad y \geqslant 1$

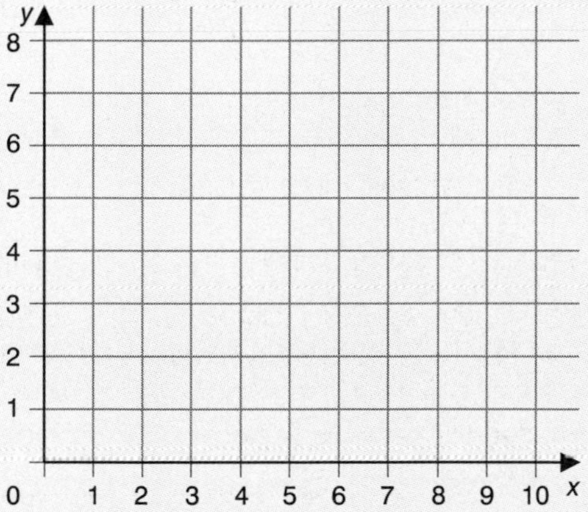

11 Find two values of x in the range $0° \leqslant x < 360°$ such that $\tan x = \sqrt{3}$.

12 a) Using the diagram, write an expression for AC².

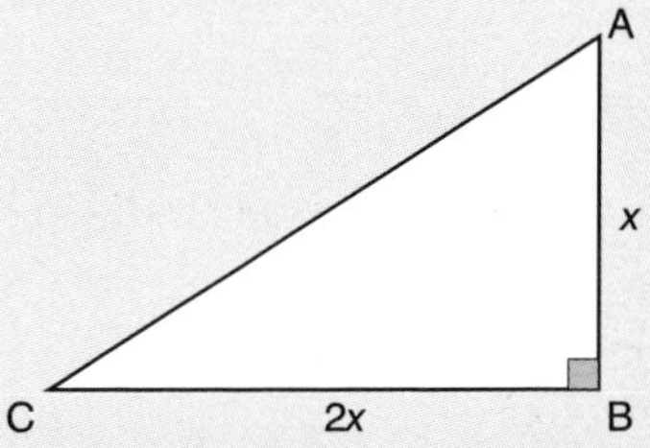

b) If AC² = 20, find the lengths of the other two sides without using a calculator. Show your working.

Answers

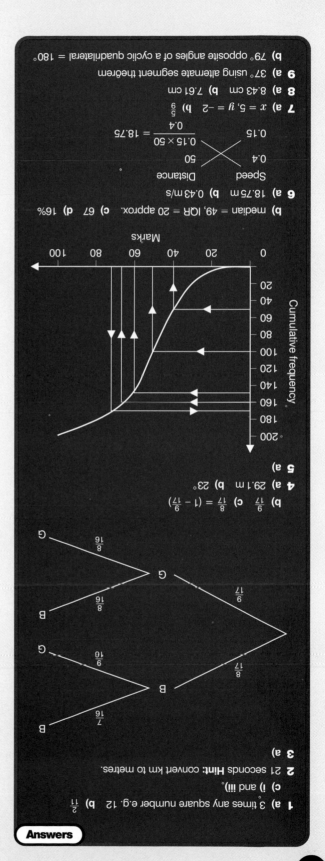

1 a) 3 times any square number e.g. 12 **b)** $\frac{2}{11}$

c) **i)** and **iii)**.

2 21 seconds **Hint:** convert km to metres.

3 a)

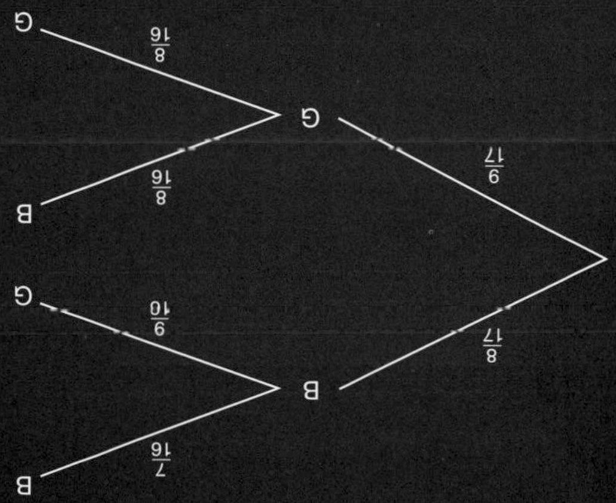

b) $\frac{9}{17}$ **c)** $\frac{8}{17} = (1 - \frac{9}{17})$

4 a) 29.1 m **b)** 23°

5 a)

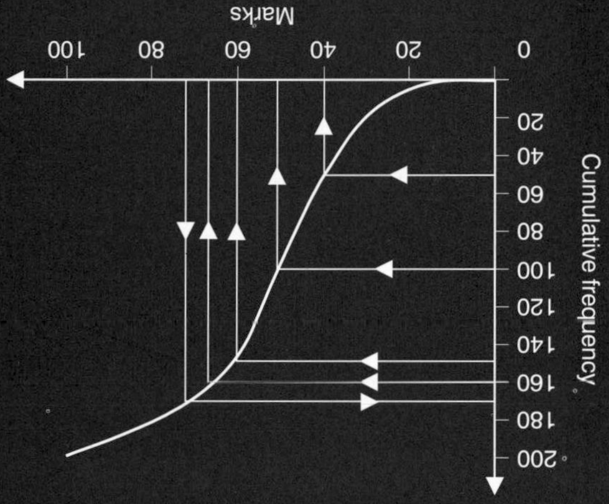

b) median = 49, IQR = 20 approx. **c)** 67 **d)** 16%

6 a) 18.75 m **b)** 0.43 m/s

Speed Distance

0.4 50

0.15 $\frac{0.15 \times 50}{0.4} = 18.75$

7 a) $x = 5, y = -2$ **b)** $\frac{5}{9}$

8 a) 8.43 cm **b)** 7.61 cm

9 a) 37° using alternate segment theorem

b) 79° opposite angles of a cyclic quadrilateral = 180°

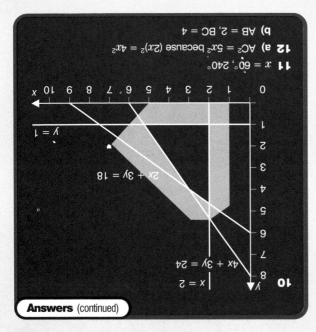

Answers (continued)

Revision in three staging posts

If you have been working through past papers, you may have noticed that some topics occur more frequently than others. Also some techniques have much wider applications than others, so you should make these topics and techniques a priority.

You can be fairly sure that you will need all the skills summarised in Stage 1, and so it clearly makes sense to master this material.

Questions involving Stage 2 information are also common, so that should be next on your revision agenda.

Stage 3 provides the icing on the cake, but could make all the difference between achieving one grade or the next.

A Sneaky Hint

As soon as possible after the first exam, write down everything that you can remember. It doesn't have to be detailed – you only need a list of the topics which were covered. Then look at your three-stage checklist, and tick off the topics that came up. If a fairly basic skill was not tested on the first paper, you can bet your bottom dollar that it will turn up on the second.

Staging posts to revision – it's as easy as 1–2–3!

Stage 1

Number
- [ ] 1 Calculator use with brackets, memory, powers and roots
- [ ] 2 Simplification involving negative and fractional powers, and surds (or roots)
- [ ] 3 Upper and lower bounds and interval approximation
- [ ] 4 Rounding and estimating to one significant figure, including problems involving square roots
- [ ] 5 Rational and irrational numbers

Algebra
- [ ] 1 Algebraic fractions
- [ ] 2 Sequences and number patterns; convergent sequences, and the idea of a limit
- [ ] 3 Simple and simultaneous equations using algebra, graphs, or trial and improvement
- [ ] 4 Quadratic equations using coefficients other than 1, factorising, iteration, the quadratic formula and combining graphs to solve equations

Shape, space and measure
- [ ] 1 Constructions and loci
- [ ] 2 Pythagoras' theorem. 2D and 3D trigonometry using right-angled triangles
- [ ] 3 Sine and cosine rules; the area of non-right angled triangles
- [ ] 4 Area and circumference of a circle; the length and area of circular arcs, sectors and segments
- [ ] 5 Scale factors and their application to length, area and volume

Handling data

☐ 1 Mean, median and mode, including those of a grouped frequency

☐ 2 Probability, including tree diagrams, mutually exclusive and independent events

☐ 3 Principles governing surveys and sampling

☐ 4 Cumulative frequency including percentiles, the median and the interquartile range

Stage 2

Number

☐ 1 Ratio, proportion and percentages. *You can usually use X-direct.*

☐ 2 Use of fractions, decimals and percentages and converting from one to another

☐ 3 Cube and cube roots of integers

☐ 4 Expressing numbers as a product of prime factors

☐ 5 Inverse proportionality graph

Algebra

☐ 1 Rearranging formulae, including powers, roots and factorising where necessary

☐ 2 The area under a graph

☐ 3 Gradient and its interpretation in real-life situations, the equation of a line

☐ 4 Tangent to a curve to determine the gradient

☐ 5 Inequalities and regions including linear programming

☐ 6 Direct and inverse variation including the use of k and in graphical form

Shape, space and measure

☐ 1 Interior and exterior angles of polygons

☐ 2 Length, area and volume; surface area and volume of a cone, cylinder or sphere

☐ 3 3D coordinates and possible combination with 3D trigonometry or Pythagoras' theorem

☐ 4 Similar shapes, possibly involving the use of algebraic fractions

☐ 5 Transformations, i.e. rotations, reflections, enlargements and translations; vectors and forces; positive and negative scale factors

Handling data

☐ 1 Other frequency diagrams, including histograms and frequency polygons

☐ 2 Standard deviation

Stage 3

Number

☐ 1 Common imperial units and their approximate metric equivalents

☐ 2 Exponential growth and decay

Algebra

☐ 1 Equation of a line where it is thought that $q = ap^2 + b$

☐ 2 Functions and composite functions

Shape, space and measure

☐ 1 Tessellation

☐ 2 Properties of a circle

☐ 3 Sin, cos or tan of any angle between 0° and 360°

☐ 4 Rules for congruent triangles

Handling data

☐ 1 Correlation

Paper 3

1 A man and a woman each invested money in a bank for ten years at a fixed rate of interest of 8.5%.
   a) The woman invested £1400.00. How much was this worth at the end of the ten years?
   b) Her twin brother received £6873.39. How much was his initial investment?

2 Two similar objects have volumes 6062 cm³ and 2458 cm³ respectively. If the surface area of the larger is 1208 cm², find the surface area of the smaller.

3 Find the values of x which satisfy the following equation.
$$2x - 1 = \frac{3}{x}$$

4 If you wanted to find out the attitude of a school population to the policy on school uniform, how would you choose a stratified random sample?

5 **a)** Find the gradient of the line $5x - 4y = 3$.
   b) Give the equation of the line parallel to $5x - 4y = 3$ which passes through the point (1, –2).

6 Match the equations to the graphs below.
   a) $y = x^3$ **b)** $y = x^2$
   c) $y = \dfrac{1}{x}$ **d)** $y = -x^2$

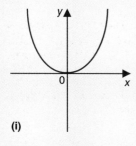
(i)

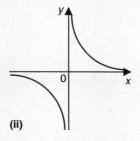
(ii)

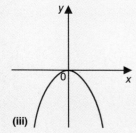
(iii)

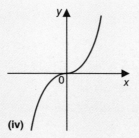
(iv)

7 A sequence is given as 3, 6, 12, 24, … .
   a) Find the 16th term of the sequence.
   b) Find a formula for the nth term of the sequence.

8 Draw a line AB of length 7 cm. Showing all construction lines, draw:
   a) its perpendicular bisector
   b) the locus of the point C where angle ACB is always 90°.

9 The dimensions of a swimming pool are shown below.

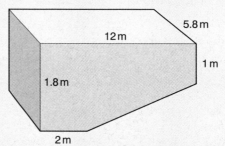

   a) Calculate the volume of the pool in cubic metres.
   b) Given that 1000 cm³ = 1 litre, convert your answer to **(a)** to litres, giving your answer in standard form.

10 What is the distance from the origin to the point with coordinates (3, 4, 7)?

11 y is inversely proportional to the square root of x. If $y = 65.7$ when $x = 2.8$, find:
   a) y when $x = 3.9$ **b)** x when $y = 52.6$.

12 **a)** Find the set of values for x which satisfy the following inequalities.
$$4x + 1 < 39 \qquad \frac{x}{6} \geqslant 1.2$$
   b) Find the largest integral value of x that satisfies these requirements.

Paper 4

1 a) Factorise fully the following expression.

$$4\pi r^2 h - 16\pi r^2 h^2$$

b) i) Factorise fully the expression $25x^2 - 1$.

ii) Hence express $\dfrac{5x + 1}{25x^2 - 1}$ in its simplest form.

2 1 litre of orange juice is poured into cylindrical glasses of base radius 2.8 cm and height 71 mm. How many glasses will be filled?

3 The graph of $y = f(x)$ is shown below. On the same axes, draw the graph of:

a) $y = f(x + 2)$ **b)** $y = f(\tfrac{1}{2}x)$.

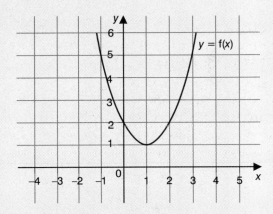

4 y is related to x by the formula $y = ab^x$, where a and b are constants. If the graph of the equation passes through the points $(0, 2)$ and $(-1, \tfrac{1}{2})$, find the value of a and b.

5 In the triangle below, which is not drawn to scale, use an algebraic method to find the value of x.

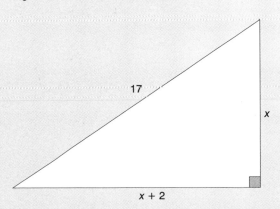

17

x

x + 2

Answers

1 a) £3165.38   **b)** £3040

2 662 cm² (Volume scale factor = 0.405, area scale factor = 0.548)

3 1.5, –1 **(Hint:** multiply both sides by x)

4 Separate the school into year groups, and take a percentage from each group which reflects the overall membership of the school.

5 a) 1.25

b) $5x - 4y = 13$

6 a) iv **b)** i **c)** ii **d)** iii

7 a) 98 304   **b)** $3 \times 2^{n-1}$

8 a)

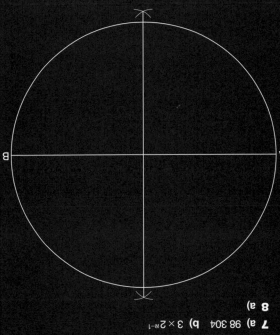

b) The locus is a circle of radius 3.5 cm with AB as its diameter. (Angle ACB forms a right angle on the circumference.)

9 a) The vertical cross-section has an area of 17.6 m² and a volume of 102.1 m³.

b) 102.1 m³ = 1.021×10^5 litres

10 8.6 (Use Pythagoras' theorem)

11 a) 55.7   **b)** 4.4

12 a) $7.2 \leqslant x < 9.5$ **b)** 9

6 The numbers of occupants per car in a survey conducted over a Saturday and a Sunday were as noted in the table below.

No. of people	1	2	3	4	5
Saturday	36	30	24	7	3
Sunday	20	25	30	17	8

a) Which day had the higher mean number of occupants?
b) Which day had the greater modal number of occupants?
c) For which day was the spread of passengers greater?

7 What straight-line graph could be drawn on the graph of the equation $y = x^2 - x$ to solve the equation $x^2 - 3x + 4 = 0$?

8 Evaluate $\dfrac{1}{p - q}$ where $p = \dfrac{1}{4.21}$ and $q = \dfrac{1}{6.84}$.
Give your answer: **i)** to 3 sig. figs. **ii)** to 2 d.p.

9 The speed-time graph of an object is shown below.

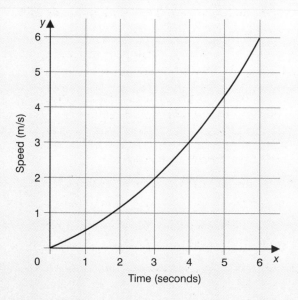

a) Showing your method clearly, estimate the acceleration of the object after 4 seconds.
b) Using the trapezium rule, and dividing the required area into three strips, estimate the distance covered by the object in 6 seconds.

10 Write $\sqrt{\dfrac{3xy}{27x^5}}$ in the form $a^{-1}x^b y^c$ stating the values of a, b and c.

11 The table shows sets of values of x and y which are related by the formula $y = ax^2 + b$. By drawing the graph of y against x^2, estimate the values of a and b.

x	0.6	0.9	1.2	1.5	1.8
y	3.6	5.1	7.3	10.2	13.6

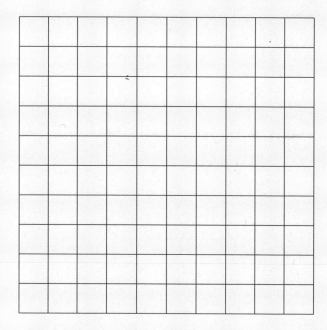

12 $-3 \leqslant x \leqslant 4$ and $-2 \leqslant y \leqslant 1$
a) What is the minimum value of xy?
b) What is the minimum value of x^2?
c) What is the maximum value of y^2?

13 The mass of the Earth is given as 5.98×10^{24} kg and the mass of Mars as 6.57×10^{23} kg.
a) Express the mass of the Earth as a percentage of the mass of Mars.
b) If the mass of Venus is given as 4.87×10^{24} kg, find the ratio of the mass of the Earth to that of Venus in the form $k : 1$. Give your answer correct to 3 sig. figs.

14 Each item of data in a sample has its value increased by 10.
a) What happens to the mean?
b) What happens to the standard deviation?

Last orders

Here is our final checklist. It is put here to jog your memory. We hope that you are now feeling much more confident about your chances. If you have stayed with us up to now, you should be.

1 Give the meanings of integer, bisect, perpendicular and vertex.

2 Sketch the HoRSe and list the conditions necessary for congruent triangles.

3 State the difference between a random and a stratified random sample.

4 How do you find the gradient of a curve?

5 How do you know whether to use the sine or the cosine rule?

6 Why might you be SoRRy not to have an ALIBI?

7 How can a CACTUS help with circles?

8 What do the m and c represent in the equation $y = mx + c$?

9 What do SEXY and STOP have to do with solving simultaneous equations?

10 How can the sign in front of the constant help you to factorise quadratic equations?

11 How do you carry out standard deviation processes on your calculator?

12 How do you find the interior angle of a regular polygon?

13 What is the difference between a histogram and a bar chart?

14 What does Con Seteenar tell you about $y = f(x)$?

15 What different transformations might you need to identify?

16 Can you recognise the graphs of $y = x$, $y = x^2$, $y = x^3$, $y = \dfrac{1}{x}$, $y = \dfrac{1}{x^2}$?

Answers

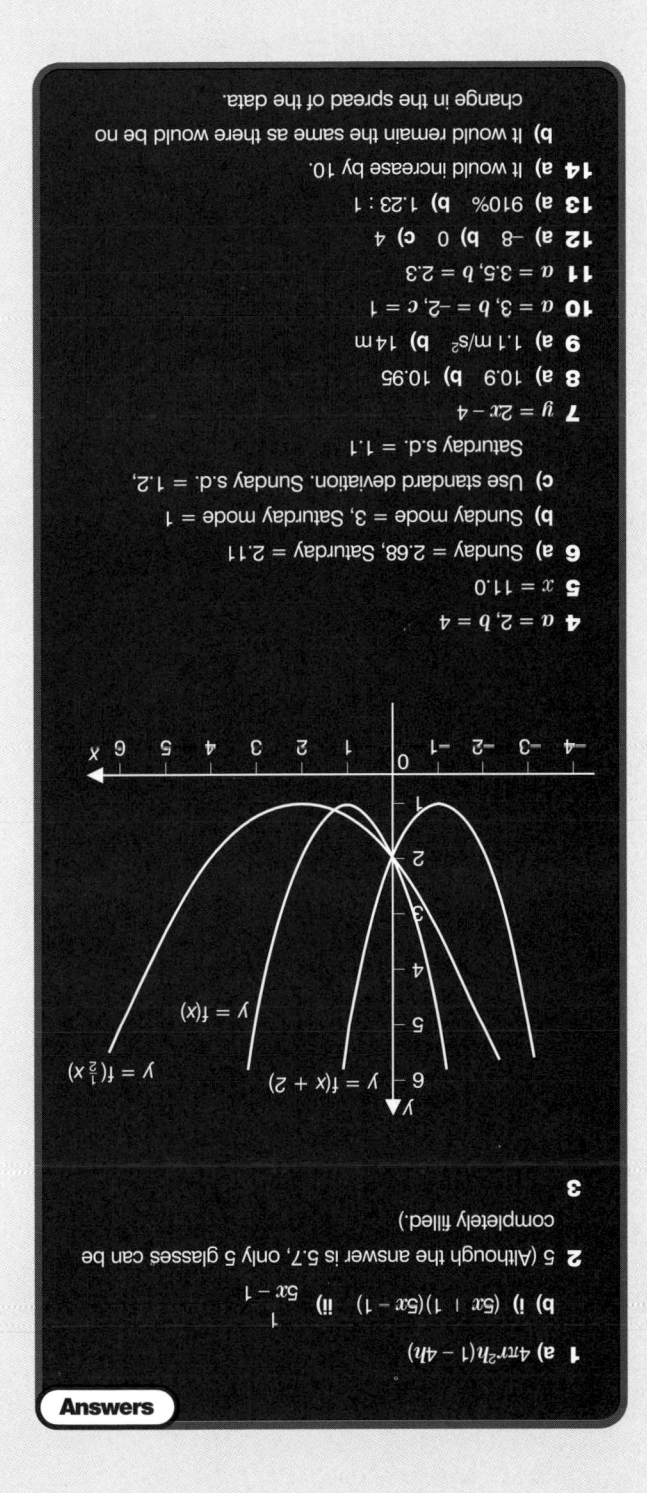

1 a) $4\pi r^2 h(1 - 4h)$
 b) i) $(5x + 1)(5x - 1)$ ii) $\dfrac{1}{5x - 1}$

2 5 (Although the answer is 5.7, only 5 glasses can be completely filled.)

3

 $y = f(x + 2)$
 $y = f\left(\frac{1}{2}x\right)$
 $y = f(x)$

4 $a = 2, b = 4$

5 $x = 11.0$

6 a) Sunday = 2.68, Saturday = 2.11
 b) Sunday mode = 3, Saturday mode = 1
 c) Use standard deviation. Sunday s.d. = 1.2, Saturday s.d. = 1.1

7 $y = 2x - 4$

8 a) 10.9 b) 10.95

9 a) 1.1 m/s^2 b) 14 m

10 $a = 3, b = -2, c = 1$

11 $a = 3.5, b = 2.3$

12 a) -8 b) 0 c) 4

13 a) 910% b) 1.23 : 1

14 a) It would increase by 10.
 b) It would remain the same as there would be no change in the spread of the data.

17 What do TIP and DIM have to do with indices, and what do x^{-1}, x^{-2}, $x^{\frac{1}{2}}$ and $x^{\frac{1}{3}}$ mean?

18 What is SOFT about a scale factor? If k is a linear scale factor, how do you find the area and volume scale factors? Also, how do you find a linear scale factor if you have the area or volume scale factor?

19 What do original sin, cos1ne and Doctor Tan have in common, and how do they differ?

20 Can you find the limit of a convergent sequence?

21 How do you know when to use SOH CAH TOA?

22 When can you use DINO to find the nth term?

23 On a scatter diagram, how can you recognise positive or negative correlation?

24 When can you not add probabilities?

25 How can you tell from the question that a quadratic equation will not factorise?

Answers

You will find many references to these topics throughout this book. We have listed some of the chapters in which they occur. Feel free to add your own notes.

1 Whole number, cut in half, at right angles, corner. (The plural of vertex is vertices.)

2 See Chapter 5.

3 A random sample is a group selected purely by chance. A stratified random sample is a group selected according to criteria and then randomly selected within that group.

4 Draw a tangent at the required point, and then complete a right-angled triangle.

5 If you are given the size of an angle, and the length of its opposite side, use the sine rule. Otherwise use the cosine rule.

6 Size, Random and Representative refer to criteria for samples. Ambiguous, Leading, Inclusive, BIased are considerations relating to surveys.

7 CACTus stands for **C**yclic quadrilaterals, **A**ngles, **C**hords and **T**angents. See Chapter 8.

8 m represents the gradient, c the y-intercept. See Chapter 3.

9 **S**imultaneous **E**quations require you to find x and y. **S**ame **T**ake **O**pposite **P**lus – a reminder for signs. See Chapter 4.

10 The sign of the constant determines the signs in the brackets. See Chapter 4.

11 Don't say you haven't been warned!

12 $\dfrac{360°}{n}$ = exterior angle;

interior angle = $180°$ – exterior angle. See Chapter 5.

13 In a histogram, frequency is represented by the area of a bar; in a bar chart, frequency is represented by the height. See Chapter 10.

14 The graph goes the opposite way to what you might expect in the x-direction. See Chapter 3.

15 Translations, reflections, enlargements and rotations. See Chapter 9.

16 See Chapter 3.

17 Times Indices Plus, Divide Indices Minus. $x^{-1} = \dfrac{1}{x}$, $x^{-2} = \dfrac{1}{x^2}$, $x^{\frac{1}{2}} = \sqrt{x}$, $x^{\frac{1}{3}} = \sqrt[3]{x}$. See Chapter 1.

18 Second Over the FirsT. k^2, k^3, $\sqrt{k}$, $\sqrt[3]{k}$. See Chapter 7.

19 They all refer to graphs of trigonometric functions. See Chapter 3.

20 Look back to Chapter 4 if you have forgotten.

21 You must have a right-angled triangle. (For all other triangles, use the sine or cosine rules.) See Chapter 6.

22 When the sequence has equal spacing between terms. See Chapter 4.

23 By the slope of the line of best fit. (If there is no line of best fit is possible, there can be no correlation.) See Chapter 11.

24 When the events are not mutually exclusive. See Chapter 11.

25 When you are asked to provide an answer correct to a number of decimal places.

Index